SHAUN RYDER

HAPPY MONDAYS, BLACK GRAPE & OTHER TRAUMAS

Published in 1997 by
INDEPENDENT MUSIC PRESS

British Library Cataloguing-in-Publication Data
A catalogue for this book is available from The British Library

ISBN 1-89-7783-11-6

Photo Credits, in order of pictures: Ian Tilton, Simon Taylor, Ian Tilton Ed Sirrs,
Martyn Goodacre, P. Allardyce, Ian Tilton, Kim Tonelli, Andy Willsher,
Hayley Madden, Peter Andersen, Steve Double, Roy Tee
Front Cover: Roy Tee   Back Cover: Simon Taylor
All photographs courtesy of S.I.N.

Independent Music Press
P.O.Box 3616, London
E2 9LN
On the Internet:
http://www.rise.co.uk/imp

SHAUN RYDER

Happy Mondays, Black Grape
And Other Traumas

by Mick Middles

Independent Music Press
London

CONTENTS

CHAPTER 1   *Fookin' 'ell man*   11

CHAPTER 2   *When we started...*   15

CHAPTER 3   *The Ryder family*   25

CHAPTER 4   *Got any draw, maaan?*   38

CHAPTER 5   *Cale And Able*   55

CHAPTER 6   *I've never bought a music paper*   65

CHAPTER 7   *I could still eat three E's a day*   71

CHAPTER 8   *We're obsessed with sex*   83

CHAPTER 9   *Madchester...faint stirrings*   87

CHAPTER 10   *America, Summer 1989, Los Angeles*   95

CHAPTER 11   *The Nasty Nineties*   100

CHAPTER 12   *March 1990*   108

CHAPTER 13   *Spring 1990, Parisian chic*   115

CHAPTER 14   *Mondays in Manhattan*   122

CHAPTER 15   *Manchester is not a nice place*   132

CHAPTER 16   *It's cheaper than water-skiing*   140

CHAPTER 17   *May 1992*   148

CHAPTER 18   *I'm not an alcoholic...*   158

CHAPTER 19   *Black Grape*   165

CHAPTER 20   *October 1995*   174

CHAPTER 21   *Imagine then*   184

CHAPTER 22   *Stormy Weather*   193

DISCOGRAPHY   197

Thanks to Richard Carman, without whom this book would never have been published.

INTRODUCTION

This book is not an exhaustive trawl through every day of the careers of Shaun Ryder, Happy Mondays or Black Grape. Having lived and worked in and around Manchester for much of my life, I wanted instead to get something of what the Mondays meant on that scene, what kind of world Ryder emerged from and what kind of world he created around him. Over the years I have bumped into all the protagonists in this odyssey many times, around Manchester, London and Paris. I have seen all the bands perform and have interviewed most of the main characters on several occasions. I have used these and other published interviews to illustrate a ramshackle tale of Rabelaisian proportions. I didn't travel to the States with the band so haven't tried to construct a diary of their time there. Instead, I have built a picture of my Mondays, of my experience of Ryder's uncompromising character and of Black Grape's emergence as a seriously good band.

The story of Shaun Ryder is one of excess, of style, of self-destruction, of being true to oneself and of coming out the other side. If Ryder himself can't remember large parts of the tale, as he readily admits, then perhaps this author can be forgiven for picking up at least some of the pieces...

CHAPTER 1

"Fookin' 'ell man, it's fookin' smart!"

With those six words, a band called Happy Mondays announced their debut appearance in the dressing room of Manchester's Hacienda nightclub. They were sharing, of course, but it mattered little. Here they were, unlikely, bedraggled ragamuffin oiks, dreamily sauntering though the Hac's backstage 'non' colours...black, silver, white, grey, black, silver, white, grey! A pristine scene, fabulously at odds with every small venue dressing room in the country. The omnipresent feint whiff of rubber, plastic, metal. The unlikely friendliness of the club's booker, Mike Pickering (what a change from the weasel-like norm of the small venue owner/booker). The sneaky scowls from the other bands and the distant faces of the sundry 'hangers on', including me, who freeloaded themselves, nightly, to the the odd beer and revelled in the kudos afforded to those who could wander, chatting to writer Jon Savage, to photographer Kevin Cummins, up and down the backstage stairs. It was fun. It was a lig. It was the centre of Manchester. A little scene. And it was the 'singer', Shaun Ryder, I think, who first discovered the beer stacked fridge that night. His fingers, for a while, delicately caressing the first bottle he plucked from the batch, like a naughty apple sapping pre-teen, let loose in a next-door neighbour's garden."

"It's like being a fookin' pop star, maan," he crowed, beaming with self importance, as the band flopped around, savouring the moment, glancing back across at the other bands, living it and loving it. Nevertheless, edging anxiously closer and closer to the dreaded moment. And, eventually, the moment came, rushing at them like some dark terror. That numbingly nerve-wracking moment when this gaggle of lads sauntered on stage, their fingers shaking noticeably as, what seemed from miles away, at the other end of the wood panelled dance floor came a tiny, pathetic muffled cheer. The Happy Mondays were on stage at The Hacienda for the first time. A golden moment? No one could possibly have known it. Even their intoxicated bravado couldn't prevent the shades of terror from showing on their faces.

From behind the bollards, from the other side of the dance floor, a few people broke their conversations and cast semi curious glances stagewards, as a loose mess of funk and rock crackled from the speakers.There was a hint, a most noticeable flashback to the early, ramshackle days of former Factory band, A Certain Ratio...days when that band would struggle and struggle and always fail to produce the fabulous innovative, sexy funk that existed in their heads - after a while, the 'struggle' would become the point of it all. Indeed, they became a huddle of lads intoxicated with Parliament, with Funkadelic, with James Brown. How could they have expected to transfer such heady influences through such inept performance? The resultant noise was spiced with frustration and yet, through the punkiness a little funk would shine through. And here, this ungainly mob from Swinton were producing a similarly hopelessly optimistic sound.

In all likelihood, the chinks of funk might well have turned a few heads, had their set been something more appealing than one quarter of a talent contest. But, as it happened, people had no real reason to spend more than a few seconds glancing stagewards, to look for something special.

*   *   *

The Hometown Gig. I didn't know the name of the band. Nobody did. It was a band. Another band...another Salford band playing on another mundane night at Manchester's Hacienda which was, even in 1984, more than just another night club. It was one of a series of 'Hometown Gigs'. An irregular, loosely organised 'talent' night, where four local bands would gather, minus the pull of a headline act, and punch their stuff across to an audience consisting of their friends, press-ganged into dutiful attendance and, perhaps, a few yawning 'Hac' regulars. (Not that the 'Hac' attracted too many regulars in those days, but those who braved the infamous 'muffled boom' were locally influential, and more often than not, on the guest list). It was a competition, of sorts, but no-one really cared who came first, or last. But, so what? It was a gig. That was good. It was something not to be sniffed at. In the Manchester of 1984, this kind of gig would either take place in Peter Street's 'The Gallery', (and this band had already exhausted that little outlet), or in blackened, back-street, cheaply hired 'gay clubs', with a cig-burned carpet and bog-like backstage, and a regular clientele of two off-duty drag queens and one optimistic fat alcoholic. The live music resurgence of the mid-eighties had yet to begin. It was one sad city, living in seemingly eternal awe of New Order, The Fall, The Smiths and, to a lesser degree, James and ACR. But it was a city that, paradoxically, generally mistrusted local bands.

As such, The Hometown Gig was, in truth, little more than an escape valve for Hacienda booker, Mike Pickering who, ever since the club opened in May 1982, had found himself wading through a relentless and artless sea of demo tapes. Bands, bands, bands...all of whom had managers whose disembodied voices would scream, more in desperation than hope, through Pickering's telephone. Each manager so keen to report back to the band that he/she had secured that all important support spot to Orange Juice, (which, strangely, always seemed to be on offer). Pickering, that rarity among club bookers, a 'genuine music fan', sensibly waived a white flag and grasped the soft option. It was a gig! What more could they hope for? He could offer some of them half an hour on the Hacienda stage, and that could never be a bad thing.

All these bands, bands, bands, with names like Awesome Precinct, Object Action, Absent Friends! Always, it seemed, four lads whose initially disparate areas of influence would funnel down to an inglorious dull groan, an all too familiar drone that would seep through the cracks of far too many practice room doors. A dour growl. The Manchester growl. A music form with a frown on its face. The Smiths minus the glittering wit. Joy Division minus the belly laughs. We, the regulars, heard far too much of it. At times it clearly clouded our judgement but we, rather than the bands, deserved some kind of prize. We suffered it every night. We clapped politely and looked for chinks of light. Occasionally and only occasionally, we thought we saw something, but then it faded back to grey and we turned around and headed back to the bar. One of the problems, in retrospect, seems so obvious. The kind of 'lads' who formed bands, would almost always be sexually repressed types, who trudged from the record shop to their bedrooms, to be forever lost in a dream world of fandom. Not at all the kind who would be bounding, god forbid, around the discos of Manchester, drunk on funk and destined for sex. No. These were dull lads. Lads who thought that Johnny Marr was rising to godlike status. How sad they were. And Mike Pickering was offering us four slabs of this at every Hometown Gig. Why did we go? Even if so few of us paid the admission fee. But, boy, how we did suffer.

There was a result that night. The band with the slightly funky bent, the ramshackle Swinton mob, were beaten into final place. Factory boss Tony Wilson did not fix it so the band would come first, as has been reported so many times. Indeed, he wasn't even at that gig. Above them, in the esteem of whoever it was who could be bothered to decide, came three bands of quite astonishing dullness. But nobody cared. No one knew, as they filed out onto Whitworth Street that night, that in time the gig they had seen would attain legendary status. It would become a noticeable footnote in the history of the club that, in turn, would become the most famous in the world. I'll be honest. I forgot all about them, perhaps just five minutes after their appearance and, had I bothered to find out who won the contest that night, or, rather, who came last, I probably wouldn't have been surprised.

CHAPTER 2

"When we started, we were shit...good, but shit.
Something had to come out of it."   Shaun Ryder

From a red tile moulding, set deep in brick above a defunct door surround in Manchester's Strangeways district, screams the words, "Manchester's Ragged School". And on a darkened rain lashed Tuesday, it's impossible not to blink back to an industrial era, when the building would be teaming with mud 'n' grime splattered children, all flashing desperate eyes and scuffed knees, numbed by the school's harsh regime, cowering in the face of full blown industrial Manchester. Schemes, themes and futuristic architectural visions by the score, have failed to erase the dark side of industrial legacy from these streets. Magnificent buildings may well have turned the heads of visiting dignitaries, just a quarter of a mile away in the city centre, but out here, in the real world, the cruel world, the pain lingers still. These streets, a rubble-scattered mess of bottom rung auto repair shops, textile and spice warehouses, are still haunted by the screamingly intense frustration of suppressed youth. Of crushed promise. Hope. Talent destroyed at seed.

How things have changed. How ironic to see such heartless suppression bubbling forth with youthful promise in the 1990's. Slap, bang in the centre of this uninspiring though evocative rubble, sits 23, New Mount Street. A fat, slab of a building - an ex-textile warehouse, no doubt -which transformed in the mid eighties into a catacomb of cheap office space, mostly dedicated, rather ironically, to nurturing youth orientated business. Music, media, design. Of all these buildings, 23, New Mount Street remains my favourite. Partly because it is a 'no frills' complex. No clever-clogs architect has imposed his particular vision here. Far from being a PR exercise, it maintains a steady ambience, from the refreshingly anti-élitist downbeat foyer to the myriad of dimly lit corridors.

Since the eighties, so much has happened in here. It was the home of the ground-breaking Sunset Radio, the first station to legally unleash hip, young, black dance music on the city before crashing, inevitably, in the face of fiscal problems and radio hierarchical battling. But from the Madchester years onwards, youthful endeavour added zip to its unlikely atmosphere, zip and a touch of glamour. It was impossible to enter, for instance, without bumping into a Stone Rose, a Charlatan, without seeing Mark E Smith scurrying into his Cog Sinister office or A Guy Called Gerald languishing on a foyer chair. It was here that an industrious Noel Gallagher would reluctantly man the Inspiral Carpets office. Add to that a whole mass of gig promoters, dance labels, fanzine scribblers, people arguing in corners, swigging from bottles of mineral water, adjourning to the pub across the road where the aforementioned Mark E Smith would, more often than not, be found in a familiar curmudgeonly huddle, chatting to 'somebody up from the *NME*. In 1996, with the Madchester fervour long hidden behind wave after wave of subsequent musical surges and lulls, 23, New Mount Street seems more sedate, a little wiser, perhaps. No longer does it feel like an excitable scramble for instant fame and subsequent riches. The optimism is still there, but it just hovers quietly while people who-feel-they-should-be-more-successful-than-they-are simply get on with their tasks.

It is in 23 New Mount Street that you will find Hot Soup Management. A little team in a frantic office, determined to nurture and reap, nurture and reap. Their justifiably optimistic efforts are topped by their credibility gaining stance as British managers of Black Grape, the most strangely likeable gang of rogues in the whole post-Britpop pile up. This is a serious, enwisened business, lacking a little of the romantic madness which prevailed nearly a decade earlier. Hot Soup's Black Grape credentials are cemented by their main man, Derek Ryder, infamous father of Shaun and Paul. Derek is an eternal evergreen on the Manchester scene, always to be found behind the mixing desks of a hundred hopefuls, always brimming with genuine enthusiasm dampened only by the cynicism that goes with extensive knowledge of the A&R scene. Derek Ryder existed for so long as the shadowy extra man on the Happy Mondays roadshow, in occasional interviews sporadically upstaging the true charismatic heart of that band, his famous son Shaun.

The 1996 vision of Derek Ryder is one of an excitable man, be-denimed and trendily bald. "It's recent," he says, slapping his pate, "I had no intention of adopting a Bobby Charlton cut, and anyway, it's always hip to be bald. Our Shaun teases me about it, though. He says I'm only doing it because I'm trying to ape that guy from The Prodigy. What a fucking cheek. I haven't got those stupid bits on the side of me 'ead, 'ave I?" Thankfully, his dome remains free from both Charlton-esque strands or Prodigy tufts, his only noticeable rock biz affectations being the studded earring which glistens from the right side of his head, and his ever excitable mobile phone. We are talking in a dank pub which has evolved from its former state of dusty, nicotine-lined den, filled with manual workers and jungle DJ's, to a new pristine, varnished theme bar. Mark E Smith, noticeably, is omnipresent no more.

Sipping Bacardi and coke, Derek Ryder displays the same downbeat demeanour as Shaun. The other give-away, naturally, is the distinctive hook nose, which curves down in a gnomic arch. He will talk forever about the current acts on Hot Soup's books. An Asian singer, from Birmingham, newly signed to Factory: "Fookin' forget Mick Hucknall, this guy, Hameed, is the best singer in Britain," he screams, as a manager should. "It's really good out there now, in the wake of Oasis. At first all the new acts sounded just like them, or like The Beatles, but it seems to have evened out recently. People are making distinctive music now, even though they are just learning to play, which is pretty healthy. We can help these bands mature in the proper way. Not like Madchester, when things happened so fast, when it all got so silly, especially within the Mondays. None of us knew what the fuck was going on. Not me. Not Shaun. Not Nathan (the manager). Not

Tony Wilson - no, especially not Tony Wilson - and don't let him tell you any different. Ahhh...he's great, Tony, really."

"You know," he continues, in motormouth form, "the Madchester thing ended in a mess and it was a great shame. There was some absolutely fantastic dance music being produced around 1990. I mean really, really classic stuff that no one had the gumption to release. It was a whole scene that just vanished because people, the record companies, just didn't understand what was happening. After the Mondays, it was as if everyone just suddenly looked away. I saw all kinds of great artists just fading to nothing. It was fuckin' tragic, really. Maybe we should shoulder some of the blame for that, I don't know. It just happened. One minute everything was up and mad an' all that, and the next...just nothing. But it is better now. Everything settled down and began to rebuild again. I think it's all really cool today. Everything is in place. Northern based A&R people are here, everything is here. The talent is all over the place, and I know, I've been around." And so he has.

Through the past, very darkly.

Derek Ryder's musical vision began as the beat boom raged in the early sixties. His favoured haunt, being the infamous nite-spot named, prophetically, Oasis. Originally a jazz club, named 2 J's, the club had spent a number of years on the fringe of Manchester's massive and unprecedented nightclub scene, strangely parallelling the city's equally legendary Merseybeat club, The Twisted Wheel (originally a beatnik cafe called The Left Wing). But the Oasis management were quick to catch onto the burgeoning pop scene, and cleverly dragged the club into the mainstream. Employing influential local DJ's such as Dave Lee Travis, Ray Teret and even, on occasion, Jimmy Saville, the Oasis policy was to forsake The Twisted Wheel's staunch R 'n' B policy and concentrate on the groups who were just beginning to battle for positions in the national music 'Hit Parade'. Hence, Oasis would soon evolve into the north's premier live music club. Its unusually plush ambience lifted it above the comparative squalor of Liverpool's internationally famous Cavern and Manchester's competing dives, Mr Smiths, The New Century Hall and the Three Coins.

"I saw The Beatles in Oasis," Ryder recalls, "and it must have been really early on because nobody really knew who they were. In fact, they didn't go down at all well because they weren't like the other bands. The thing was, in those days, if you were in a group, you had to produce an exact copy of what was in the charts. That was the point. That's how you were judged. If you were regarded as a good band it meant that you sounded like the groups in the charts. People expected an exact copy and groups would make considerable reputations just by that ability. It was almost like the tribute bands in a sense, because you would get the music second-hand. Human jukeboxes. I remember, as a struggling musician, believing that to copy a chart sound would be the absolute ultimate achievement. Nobody was in the least bit interested in a band who came along and played their own material. Well, maybe they were, in the R 'n' B clubs, but not in Oasis. It was odd. I think that people really thought that people who were stars were kind of untouchable and they were perfectly happy to see a band produce a duplicate sound. I think that, although the British bands had broken through, the crowds were still in a state of throwback from the old days when rock 'n' roll stars still came from America. Well, it wasn't just America, but it was certainly *somewhere else*. They didn't come from around the corner.

"That is why The Beatles didn't go down at all well in the early days of Oasis, simply because they broke the mould. They came on and played all these new songs - nobody wanted that. Who the hell did they think they were? It was funny. It wasn't the audience's fault, they simply didn't know how to judge music they hadn't heard before. I distinctly remember people saying, "The Beatles are crap, they can't play." Well, they could play but people didn't know what guitar line was supposed to come next. It had never happened before, had it? So how could people know what was good and what wasn't? They had no critical faculties. It was that basic."

Not that such a peculiar local 'non-scene' would stop Derek Ryder from taking musical chances of his own. Taking a lead from the bands he saw at Oasis, he would sing and play bass in bands and as a solo performer, as a musician and a pub comic. At the time the north west gig circuit was bewilderingly complex, stacked with tiny venues, pubs, clubs, youth clubs, cafe's, scout huts, all offering both lunchtime and evening single gigs and residences. Controlling this rather loose scene would be a vulturous gang of inter-connected agents, many of whom would think nothing of pushing a lowly act through up to forty or fifty performances per month.

"Yeah, the agents were in place but I was never involved in all that," states Derek, "I stayed pretty local, on the Salford pub and Mecca circuit. It was dead simple, really, If a landlord liked you one week, he'd book you for the next. You'd just turn up and play. I had a band up and running for a while. In fact, when I think about it, it must have been very early indeed. The scene at the time was pretty much like it is today, in the sense that there was a circle of unknown and unsigned bands who would be constantly attempting to get their friends and families to attend the gigs. Unsigned acts like Freddie And The Dreamers and The Hollies. I knew all those people before they broke but, because it had never happened before, I don't think anyone really expected big things to happen. But they did, so it was confusing for everyone. That line between getting somewhere, becoming famous, and failing was practically impossible to see. And when big things happened to a band, nobody really believed it at the time. It didn't seem possible."

Big things, however, didn't happen to Derek Ryder, though he fell effortlessly onto an increasingly surreal Salford pub circuit, playing mainly covers and attempting to impress a clientele who wallowed in various degrees of disinterest, seediness and occasional downright aggression. These were venues of a dark, nicotine-stained kind, where acts played a supporting role to King Bingo which, at least, offered a small degree of hope. This was a Salford that was, literally, being smashed into rubble as the mighty wave of apparently liberating slum clearance crashed its way through the city's tightly knit web of camaraderie. In the early to mid-sixties, the personality of Salford suffered a virtual lobotomy as architectural and governmental idiocy snapped the city's pride in half. Salford - perhaps the first casualty of mindless political correctness.

Not that Derek Ryder worried too much. He rode the inevitable collapse of Merseybeat with ease and wasn't at all concerned about Manchester's shrinking nightclub scene. By the time that a blue clad Manchester United were holding the European Cup aloft at Wembley, Derek Ryder was drifting around the psychedelic hovels of Manchester's Magic Village, his hair falling in corkscrews down both sides of his face. Afghan-coated, loon-panted, adrift on a wave of chemical assistance, Derek Ryder attempted, and succeeded, in attaining the Ian Hunter look, the late sixties look, the look of progressive awareness. He wasn't a hippy, not ever...but he was hip, man.

Shaun Ryder on Derek Ryder: "To be honest, me Dad, he was one of those working class geezers who tried loads of things and they never seemed to work out for him. It was only with us that he finally came good. He always wanted to get on the road, so we finally gave in and let him drive the van. He'd be away from mum for months. You should have seen 'im when he got to New York, running all over the fuckin' place, "acquiring" things. He was completely caned out of his shed. That's where a lot of our early equipment came from."

Shaun would remain, albeit secretly, rather proud of his Dad's spirited under-achievements. This was evident in January 1991 when, on the plane heading home from the infamous Rock In Rio event, Shaun approached a startled Lisa Stansfield, who had appeared at the same show.

Lisa Stansfield: "Oh god, yeah, I remember that. We were dead worried about Happy Mondays, 'cos we thought they would regard us as too poppy or something. We spotted Shaun walking down the aisle towards us. I was dead nervous, but he was really, really sweet. Almost fawning. And he told me that he had always wanted to meet me, especially because, apparently, I had once beaten his Dad, a pub comic, into second place. He said that his Dad was always going on about it. I can't remember it to be honest, but if he had been on the same bill as me, it must have been a right bloody shit-hole."

Dickensian Oiks

Shaun and Paul Ryder spent their childhood prowling the streets of Little Hulton, from the family home in Coningston Avenue. A road adrift in a housing estate where individuality is suppressed by the faceless stares of a thousand yellow houses. A childhood veering on, and often dipping deeply, into areas of staggering juvenile criminality. The place hasn't changed. As Shaun would later state "Kids from 13 to 19 are walking time bombs where I come from, from the council estates of Swinton. Psychotic bastards. I'd lock 'em up. We've all been in the nick for this an' that. So what? It's a way of life where I come from. You go out, rip off cars, nab things, fuck things up. It isn't looked upon as criminal, it's just like...it's life. It's what people are supposed to do and, frankly, it's all we knew."

Sadly, it is and it was. In retrospect, Shaun Ryder now regrets large chunks of his childhood. Attaching mice to gas pipes and blowing them up. Shaun Ryder managed to murder all his science teacher's animals, one by one. He's not happy about that now but people mature. But, for such a long time, more than his brother, and more than Bez as well, Shaun Ryder seemed an archetypal 'hopeless case'. Falling fast into hopeless chemical dependency.

Chemicals, however, could not be held responsible for the morning when a 15 year old Shaun Ryder was walking along Hilton Lane, in Little Hulton, vaguely intent on catching the 7am school bus. Accompanied by a school mate, Ryder froze stock-still in terror, gazing at the sky where, to this day, he swears he saw a UFO. As recently as February 1997, in *Select* magazine, he would proclaim, "...and we saw this thing that just goes, pher-chung! Chung! Chung! Pwa! Pow! It was a glowing thing and we're watching and it was looking at us. Then, Chuunnn! It was gone." A close encounter? In Little Hulton? What would *they* have made of us? Ryder remains convinced. "I've seen a few things but people are always 'You're on drugs', when you see a fuckin' UFO on the tennis courts in Didsbury. But I know what I've seen. And they watch you. Once they see you, they do keep a check on you. I reckon we made contact with them in the sixties."

A Friend For Life

Shaun Ryder met Mark 'Bez' Berry down at the dole office. The meetings were scorched with the frisson of being penniless and being alive, of being secretly ambitious while in the eyes of society being regarded as aimless, wandering, hopeless cases. Drug addicts most probably, ungifted, untalented, inelegant, undignified, undeserving, dangerous. Bez had been thrown out of his house, by his father, a C.I.D. Inspector. Shaun later referred to him in the *NME* in this generous manner: "A right cunt he was. Bez would have to sneak into the dole 'cos if his Dad saw him, he'd come out of the house and fucking beat him up, hammer him. The guy is an evil Scouse fucking pig." He continued "I'd say 'out, me, to make our lives seem interesting. I'm a right gobby bastard." The above sentence rather succinctly, if inelegantly, sums up the state of the playmates' minds as they wandered regularly along the deadening Cemetry Road in Swinton, seeking something more. Which is all they ever wanted.

Ryder took his first 'proper' drug at the age of thirteen. Acid. A microdot. He wasn't that thrilled. Tripping furiously, high on a cloud, he drifted through the streets of Salford, floating, honing in on conversations seemingly taking place miles away.

Once he had teamed up with Bez, they were soon taking three or four at a time, more in an effort to break the sheer tedium of a penniless Salfordian teenage life than anything else. They'd take them together, wait for the buzz to build, and then walk down to Manchester's ugly Arndale Centre. Unlikely as it may sound, it was during these stoned meanderings that Bez developed his curious underwater style of dancing. There he was, on Bury New Road, wading through the fog of his acid trip, everything in slow motion, everything ever-so slightly day-glo. Everything strangely sound-tracked by an ambient mush. The source of Happy Mondays, it may be presumed, lay back there, smack bang in those juvenile acid trips.

CHAPTER 3

The Ryder family's background has been etched, in rather comedic manner, into Little Hulton folklore by Shaun himself, who has often stretched the characters into caricature. "Most of our family were fucking alkies," he would state, "loads of them died from drink related things. It was always, 'have a drink...have a drink' in our house. God, me Gran smokin' dope an' that. And me Grandad. He were called Big Billy Carroll. One big, Irish motherfucker, cock of the estate. He was a bit of a spiv. He'd go to church every fuckin' night, say a prayer, and then be up to his old fuckin' ways. There was lorry drivers around the way lost their jobs 'cos Big Billy had turned their lorries over. He always had crates and crates of Newcy Brown in the shed."

The big gang of Shaun and Paul's would soon be swelling into the pubs and then the clubs of Manchester. From there it would extend around the world in a thousand crazed sortés in the wildly shambolic tours of Happy Mondays. At this point, it remained largely contained within the most northerly areas of Salford. Although hardly close pals, Shaun had often seen Gary Whelan and Paul Davis darting about and, more often than not, falling into profoundly delinquent activities. Indeed, he had first noticed the final Monday, Mark Day at the age of six. Ryder was trundling along on his bike when he spotted this bizarre looking kid, with, in Shaun's words, "a dead little body but a massive big head." Mark Day, in time, would attend Wardley High School along with Gaz, Paul Davis and Mark Berry. The Ryder's, however, attended Ambrose, ten minutes walk away. Never one to fall prey to academia, Shaun Ryder was always one of those kids who might spend the rest of their lives justifiably claiming to have been "too bright" for the education system. Ryder would always be the one to doubt the teachings, to challenge the so-called 'facts' that were chalked before him. A teacher's nightmare, he would never accept the system, play it to his advantage, and meekly buckle down to the task in hand. Instead, his intelligence funnelled down into becoming the class clown, into entertaining his more studious but less gifted schoolmates, a trait he inherited directly from his father. Any artistic leanings would be reserved for dinner time, when he would conjure up a thousand highly juvenile methods of asking for chips, peas and gravy at the local chippy: Swinton rhyming slang. "Rabbit poo with chips 'n' spunky gravy, please." Occasionally, he tried slamming a few words down on paper but, alas, would do little more than draw unfeasibly large penises on pictures of the celebrities of the day. Although later he would proudly state that he never read a book at school, he did actually spend time with his nose inside some garish Sven Hassell macho novel. He devoured the works of Richard Allen, Skinhead, Suedehead, Skinhead Escapes et al. The life, times and cheap thrills of the West Ham supporting Joe Hawkins proved irresistible to him, and installed a mod-like love of street clothes. Crombie overcoats, Levi Stayprest trousers, brogues, Barathea Blazers, two tone tonic suits. Although rather on the young side to catch the full blown, post-skinhead 'Crombie wars' of Manchester and Salford (at the time no bus station was free of the sounds of scuffling leather souls and battling 'suedes') Ryder was hugely affected by the fashion which featured so heavily in the generation above him. His love of clothes, his lustful tendency to be a "right flash git" stems directly from such times. Times when the measure of a lad would be the cut of his Crombie. Not the cheap teen fashion trash one could purchase from Oasis in Manchester's notorious Underground Market. To be truly cool was to wear the real McCoy.

Shaun left school at 15 and before long he took up his position, as his father had, working for the Post Office. Derek would pound the beat, pulling in £100 a week while Shaun, deliberately and mischievously, failed to progress past the post of messenger boy. The notion of falling into a lifelong career delivering letters terrified him and he left before he was 18, the age when you are upgraded to become a *bona fide* postman.

"Being a messenger had been a laugh," he would state, "we used to deliver telegrams and generally just fuck around, but I would see these guys, year in, year out, trudging through Swinton, bags piled high. They were good guys, I liked them, but I thought that their lives were becoming increasingly sad, year after year. That path was only too open to me. It was expected of me, in a way, but I had enough of me Dad in me to know that I wanted something better. I wasn't sure what, but I wasn't going down that road. No way."

Stealing cars, smashing cars, stealing this and that, messing about, swallowing the drugs which were swirling about the streets of Salford, was regarded as juvenile distraction in those pre-smack days before low grade gangster society darkened the entire scene. This was still a time when such activities seemed the sharp end of teenage mischief, a dark place from which, eventually the young Ryder might return....and be a postman for evermore.

*   *   *

Bez: "I keep going too fast, like. I keep getting in it and I drive like, dead normal and I just start getting bored. You know what I mean? I'm burnin' down the road at 120 miles an hour, wooooarrrghhhhh! In and out of traffic, can't even stop at traffic lights, man, they bore me stupid. I've been like that since I were a kid."

The last car that Shaun stole was a Ford Granada. A mighty monster of a vehicle, a sales reps dream. The car was brand new, shimmering like a jewel on the side of the East Lancs Road. Impossible to pass by. Shaun slipped stealthily behind the wheel, fired up the monster and hurtled, in the manner that only teenagers can, down that dreamlike road. Immediately, of course, a police car attached itself to his tale and Shaun, in a mild panic, swung the beast right and then left, into a waiting cul-de-sac, before hurtling the thing straight through a wall and the privet hedge beyond. Ryder, heavily "bladdered", staggered from the car out onto the lawn where a startled elderly couple had been engaged in a spot of topiary. Unluckily for Ryder, their beloved son happened to be a local policeman.

Funk, punk, stun and dent!

The shambolic rumble of sordid camaraderie, teen angst, fumbling, artless musicianship, gibbering Salfordian street-speak, impenetrable in-jokes punctuated by relentless vulgarities, profound hedonism, strange and deep rooted musical knowledge and mod-ish sports gear casual fashion...this was all that would become Happy Mondays. It began when Shaun Ryder was stagnating in the deadening dole queue, drifting around the edges of serious criminality and worshipping local heroes who were little more than loser-bound psychotic thugs. Going nowhere and slowly sinking further and further into the surrounding grime, becoming part of the sorry landscape. It was, it seemed, the only path open to him, other than spending his life with a post bag attached to his back. There was the aforementioned seed of ambition, but, while it had been planted by his father it had, equally, been stifled by Derek's own failure to break through the grime in the sixties and seventies. Derek had slowly sunk back into drudgery, watching a few of his musicianly friends drifting up and away, although most of them would return eventually to an increasingly sad area of downmarket cabaret. All those years, all those attempts, those near misses. That classic tale of Merseybeat, that time when great, unheard of riches flashed so unexpectedly before the eyes of the likes of Derek Ryder...and then, tragically, away. All this had flowed down into the psyche of young Shaun. He couldn't have known it then, and he probably couldn't dare to recognise it, but his Dad's struggle had fired a brooding determination. Somewhere, deep down in Shaun Ryder, lay a most unlikely winner.

Shaun was 19 when it all began. When Gaz Whelan and Paul Davis were still entrapped at Wardley High School, it sort of fell together, messily, which is exactly how it would continue. Paul Davis, for example, his head swilling with rumours about this local band, approached Shaun on the street one day, uttering the words "Is Gaz Whelan in your band? I know him. He's my best mate but he's shit. He shouldn't be in your band. What does he do? Play drums? He's crap at that. I can do it better than him. I can play anything he can. Put me in your band, get rid of him...I wanna be in it."

At the next practice, taking place in an old school hall, Shaun informed Gaz Whelan that Paul Davis might be turning up. The effect was startling, with Gaz instantly swaying onto the defensive, slagging Paul with an unbecoming vengeance and threatening to walk out. Shaun wasn't too worried. After all, Davis had been fired by sheer bravado and, when it actually came down to it, the chances were that he would do the decent thing and bottle out. But to Gaz's chagrin, and to Shaun's distress, Paul Davis duly turned up, excited and keen to begin. In his arms he was carrying a small, dated and mostly useless keyboard and so, if only to keep the peace, Shaun instructed him to sit in the corner and play it. Unfortunately, and perhaps not surprisingly, he was no Rick Wakeman. He wasn't even Bobby Crush, although Ryder warmed to his sheer, unflinching and rather blind enthusiasm and naiveté. It wasn't to last. One week later, Paul Davis would turn up without the tinky keyboard, but this time carrying a bass guitar."

"You are not fucking well playing that," Shaun informed him, assuming the mantle of leader, "Our kid plays bass, you knew that! What are you trying to do, split us up. Go and play your fuckin' keyboards."

For a while, Shaun and Paul Ryder would share a flat with Bez in Salford. By all accounts it was an abode which, once inside, became difficult to navigate. The kitchen for example was "behind all that stuff, there." From this flat the loveable trio would sell draw, dope, skag. Nothing worse but, they would later boast, the best, the meanest skag around. A rather unofficial activity which helped them pile together enough "readies" to assemble band equipment. The neighbourhood was a perfect marketplace for them, being simply awash with dope-head ex-musicians looking for some kind of hit. These musicians would bring along little pieces of band equipment, a DX7 keyboard, for example, which would be all too hastily swapped for half an ounce of weed. A bargain! The next week, the skanked out muso's would be back, optimistically holding a spaghetti mess of leads in front of them. Before long the flat would resemble a second-hand electrical warehouse. It was manned by Shaun and Bez who, once they'd cashed their fortnightly Giros ("What's green and gets you pissed?"), would simply sit around doing drugs all day.

"We'd stare at the telly or the sideboard, just vegin-out," stated Bez, "we never really had much ambition, we never saw beyond those four walls. Just think, we could very easily still be in there now." As a way of life, it had its limitations, but the frustration gathered during the day would soon begin to filter out through Ryder's increasingly interesting lyric writing. Words that would find themselves scrawled across discarded fag packets or on the rear side of DHSS forms. To Shaun Ryder's immense surprise, and, indeed, to his eventual relief, he discovered that he *could* write. All he had to do next was to convince everyone around him. That, he reasoned, wouldn't be easy at all.

Street life

With Shaun simply firing daft, nonsensical lyrics, pulled from street chat, school jokes, pub natter and everyday lapses into plain old juvenile lunacy, the band edged towards surrealism. Their real names, for example, were hastily jettisoned. Shaun had already become locally known as X, and the name would stick. Typically, this minuscule monicker had its origins in the local drugs scene. When Shaun had been eighteen, he would sell draw in Manchester clubs and, in order to warn him of approaching officials, his friends warning shouts of "Shaun" would soon be whittled down to the rather more coded "X". Pretty soon, whenever Shaun strode into view, friends would immediately begin shouting "X" in a light-hearted attempt to drive Shaun into paranoia. Paul Ryder's nickname, Horse, is a little more difficult to pin down. The name had originally belonged to Shaun while still at school, although this was strangely shunted across to Derek Ryder who became known as Horseman - he had briefly adopted this name in the seventies after America's sardonic desert song 'Horse With No Name'. Eventually, and probably because people would joke that Paul Ryder was "hung like a horse", he gleefully adopted the nickname. For reasons that are frankly rather obvious, Paul Davis didn't seem to complain when people started calling him first Knobhead, then later Penis. Mark Day spent much of his teenage years under the guise of Cow or Moose, or Bastard or Daisy...take your pick. Rather less cryptically, Gaz was known for a while as Ronny, after the Liverpool footballer, Ronny Whelan.

Club Life

Manchester's Pip's Disco, which nestled sweetly in the shadows of the city's eternally disappointing cathedral was arguably the most catalytic and influential club in Manchester's music history. It had earned its initial reputation as the appropriately named Nice 'n' Easy in the sixties which, although hardly a predecessor of the Easy Listening venues of the nineties, provided a softer alternative to the harsh R'n'B which flourished in the wake of Merseybeat. For a while, it softened further until it became a natural magnet for the handbag clasping office girls who would swirl around its numerous dance floors to the just breaking and innovative early disco. Somewhere along the line, however, something clicked with the management who previously had failed to show any aptitude for innovation. Here was a club that was positively the antithesis of the cavernous cinema-cum-bingo-cum-dance halls that typified the aloof and blistering northern soul outbreak. Here was a catacomb club, a mish-mash of rooms, bars and corridors. People liked to go into the club and simply melt into the shadows. Once re-opened as Pips, it soon became clear that this place could offer a disparate mixture of music forms, attracting club go-ers from right across the musical spectrum. Alongside the smootchy lover-soulies was the infamous Roxy Room, full of spandex clad Bowie freaks, who would moan and pout furiously, camping it up to the sound of Lou Reed, The Velvets, Iggy, New York Dolls and the best and worst examples of British glam. Strangely, although this 'freak room' (as it became known) was situated literally feet away from a swirling cavern of northern soul and even, at one point, a smokey den of progressive rock, there was very little trouble.

Happy Mondays, like practically all the Manchester bands who would break in the ten years which followed the punk explosion, spent endless hours drifting through Pips, settling for a while in the darkness of the Roxy Room, before splitting and winding through the nine rooms, each blasting a different noise, a different vision, at times with differing sexual persuasions as well. In Pips you could meet and chat to a rum-and-black-fuelled temp with a neat line in soul dancing and a parent-free house waiting back in Handforth. Or you could, and often did, find yourself chatting naively away to some creature of unidentifiable gender, filled with unholy intent. Clearly, the Mondays were hugely affected by the Pip's New York experience, and their first album would, in so many ways, reflect the distant atmosphere of that club. In the early eighties, the band's record collections would swell with the usual indie stiff, Joy Division, Bunnymen and New Order, through to the white soul of Orange Juice, to dance and funk, stopping along the way to cast a casual nod towards the Stones and Beatles albums that rested dustily in their parents' record collections. Stack that lot together, add alcohol, dope and a mass of local chatter and gossip and you have Pips. You also have Happy Mondays.

The Twenty Four Hour Party People

Phil Saxe, owner of the 'Some Wear' clothes stall in Oasis centre, (known mostly for its range of street shoes) was already well known on the local scene as an entrepreneur-cum-hassle and haggle merchant and, perhaps even more importantly, an eminent northern soul DJ. He hung around with local notables such as Richard Searling, the legendary soul DJ and early supporter of Joy Division, and with Mike Pickering, part time A&R man for Factory Records. He found the Mondays, initially, as a horrible heap of bumping bones and sweat, bouncing around the bollards of the Hacienda dance floor. Always on the lookout for a band to manage - he's on the lookout still - he encouraged their confidence, and their instant like for him grew considerably as he allowed them to spend their days hanging around his shop skinning up, while listening to and talking about music. Although nothing formal was agreed, Phil Saxe seemed like a natural choice for manager even before he successfully secured them a lowly gig at Manchester's The Gallery.

This was a tiny, theatre-like venue run by Saxe's friend, the enigmatic Peter Gresty, a full blooded music enthusiast and latter-day taxi driver who frequently allowed his passion to stand in the way of his rather sordid role as small venue booker. Occasionally The Gallery would be bursting at the seams to the likes of Marillion, The Alarm, The Armoury Show and The Tube Roadshow but more often than not it was empty, soulless and sad. Naturally, this is how it was for the Happy Mondays. Just a a trickle of friends, helpers and family members showed up, all too stoned to notice the band anyway.

For Saxe, selling clothes was a way into the psyche of Manchester's street youth, an peek at the ebbs and flows of working class fashion. He always found it infinitely more interesting to watch the little gangs congregate in the darkened corners of the ugliest shopping mall in the world, than to see the Doc Martin-shod, overcoat-clad, baggy-shirted students thronging through the downmarket bohemia of Afflecks

Palace where the waft of grilled lentil burgers mingled with the omnipresent cloud of incense. But Phil Saxe was never, really, an Afflecks-style, Bohemian-biased entrepreneur. Like Joe Moss, clothes-selling early manager of The Smiths and Crazy Face, he favoured the sharper, neater, mod-ish street vision. Saxe pushed Happy Mondays onto everyone...local venue owners, promoters and aspiring journalists from *City Life* and *Muze, Sounds, NME* and *Melody Maker, South Manchester Reporter* and the *Manchester Evening News*. He began to attract the tag 'the Malcolm McLaren of the perry boys' ('perry boys' being a kind of Manc version of Liverpool's infamous 'scallies'). The tag wasn't wholly unsuitable, for he achieved a Fagin style eminence. Like most of the luminaries who flitted around the Manchester scene, (The Stone Roses manager Gareth Evans or even Factory boss Tony Wilson himself), Saxe always gave the impression that there was some kind of hidden agenda. This was especially apparent when he was surrounded by his foot soldiers - who better than Happy Mondays to assist him in evoking such Dickensian imagery, grubby street urchins, petty pilferers, loveable rogues to a lad. More often than not, the band would sit around in stony silence (though not as gormlessly silent as The Stone Roses, the worst interview band of all time), and inevitably Saxe would fall merrily into the role of tap room philosopher.

"That footballer, Socrates," he once blandly stated, "he doesn't half look like you imagine the original Socrates must have looked. Put him in a toga and he'd be identical. Actually, the ancient Greeks used to walk around naked. I've seen it on vases. Not the modern Greeks, they sodomise sheep. No, they do! It was in that film, *All You Wanted To Know About Sex But Were Afraid To Ask*. I saw it in this book of sex slang. I love those books, like books of lists, where you are staggered to find out that Ronnie Corbett's got size 15 feet!"

This chunk of minutiae is from an early interview with the band when the journalist was forced to swing the conversation away from the assembled band, and towards the ever-talkative manager. In this case, after allowing this little pearl to snap the spell of band silence, Shaun Ryder would illuminate the outburst with the admiring, though hardly eloquent "That's funneh!", delivered, of course, in his finest Salfordian drawl. At one interview attended by this writer, Saxe compensated for the band's lack of enthusiasm by drawing tiny, but rather vivid descriptions of each band member.

"There's Shaun, the singer," he would point out, as the shaven haired, goatee bearded Ryder would break into a mock angelic beam, "and there's Gaz, who has dreams about making love to girls who turn into dogs and hiding them behind his settee. Then there's Paul, who keeps trying to come and live in my house. When I had an extension built, I swore the group to secrecy so that he wouldn't be round with his bed. It's not all good times," he continued, "sometimes we have arguments. I threw a can of beer at Shaun once...and missed."

Prestbury, Cheshire, Summer 1985

There must have been fifteen of them. Tumbling out of the Admiral Rodney, an oak beamed hostelry, more usually filled with retired captains of industry, or guffawing middle class post grads, than this be-denimed mess of rock fans, full of swearing banter and bright anticipation. They had travelled into Cheshire, from Gorton, Denton, Salford and Hulme, to catch a rare performance by their beloved New Order. A gig taking place, as far as they were concerned, "somewhere in the bleedin' countryside." The venue was difficult to locate, and on arrival was the featureless shell called Macclesfield Leisure Centre. A cubic mass of tedious brick and breeze block. But these fans, intent on enjoying themselves, flitted in and out of Prestbury's couple of gentrified pubs, causing enough commotion to ignite the outrage of the locals, whose letters stormed onto the back page of the *Macclesfield Express*, screaming for the blood of the city-ites who had threatened to disrupt the village's locally-celebrated prettiness.

This was the gig, an infamous gig really, when many of us

first, knowingly, came face to face with the band called Happy Mondays. We had no idea who they were. Indeed, upon receiving our tickets, and scanning the words, *"Plus Support - Happy Mondays"* most of us instantly recognised as a 'Blue Monday' antithesis, and assumed it would be some kind of electronic New Order joke. A film, maybe, or some kind of arty video. It came as quite a surprise, therefore, to discover that the band called Happy Mondays were, in fact, that same scruffy bunch who had finished in last place at the Hacienda Hometown Gig. "Oh...it's them!" I remember stating, as they stumbled on stage, looking lost in the vastness of the leisure centre, casting nervous glances this way and that, fumbling through bass lines, thumping an irregular snare pattern. They fell into a set that had somehow departed from the musical trajectory of early A Certain Ratio. It was a groove, rather than a collection of songs, a groove that faded to a halt every six minutes or so and, after several seconds embarrassed silence, filled by more school kid nervous glances, kicked into gear once again. After a while there seemed to be a genuine, recognisable shape to the funk even if the singer often tended to forget the limitations of his voice and launched into a vocal that had no noticeable links with the music beneath. Nevertheless, it was probably as much fun as one could have while watching an unknown band in a soul-less leisure centre. Had we known that lazy old New Order would take two whole hours to reach the stage, we probably would have shouted for more. We might have even danced a little. It wasn't our fault that we failed to sense the potential within that rabble, for it would have taken ears of acute and rare perception to have sensed anything other than a set packed with spirited dullness. Notably, New Order's inimitable bass player, Pete Hook, had inexplicably fallen head over heals in love with this strange grumbling funk. "There are a few decent bands around, now," he mistakenly announced at Macclesfield, "But that lot, Happy Mondays, are the best I've seen. They are going to be massive." Well, I didn't believe that for one minute. Massive? How come? What was in there that might separate the Mondays from the masses? I couldn't tell and, frankly, I put Hooky's seemingly absurd appraisal down to sheer Factory braggadocio.

CHAPTER 4

"Got any draw, maaan?"

Following the band's set, something strange happened. It was something that, for the next year at least, would become a regular feature of a Happy Mondays gig. At least a couple of members of the band would filter into the crowd, circulating, as if observing social etiquette at their own wedding party. I can see their faces now - not at all threatening, in fact rather sweet. The hangdog face of Shaun Ryder, twisted with apparent pain, launching into one of the two questions with which his name would become synonymous, "Hey, have you got any draw, maan?" or "Hey, do you want some draw, maan?" Well, I never knew what to say. Would you buy draw from a man with a hook nose and a sardonic leer? Plenty of people did. Then, off he/they would scurry, a conspiratorial huddle of Manc chat and in-jokes. A funny lot. All heads-down and insular, like a school yard gang. Happy Mondays - I didn't know what the hell to make of them at first to be honest and my confusion was shared by most people who happened to bump into them.

I was to see the Happy Mondays a lot during the next eighteen months. In fact, I was to see more of them than any other band during what was, thanks to the vigorous efforts of venues like The Boardwalk and The International, quite the healthiest grass routes local rock scene in Manchester history. At the time, I had started writing a local rock column, 'The Word', in *The Manchester Evening News* as well as editing a fairly lumbering glossy music monthly called *Muze*. No big deal but, as hardly any of the local acts - including The Stone Roses, James et al - could barely get a mention in the national music press, they all seemed to tumble towards me with desperation in their eyes. Apart, that is, from Happy Mondays, who only seemed to want to sell or buy dope! They were different. I'm sure behind those sad, pleading eyes raged a furious ambition and competitive spirit, but it never seemed to surface. Happy Mondays just seemed to get on with being Happy Mondays. That was it. A way of life, for better or worse, as successes or as failures. The rest of Manchester had fallen into an exciting but somewhat sordid scramble for press attention, indeed for any kind of attention at all. Not the Mondays. Their gigs could be a stunning sweat-soaked dance groove or they could be as flaccid as a Lord Mayor's parade. Like most who floated about the Manchester scene, I nurtured a love/hate relationship with their music. I recall being rather dumb-struck upon discovering just how the Factory Records personnel had fallen hook, line and sinker for this funny little band. Indeed, Factory's early love for the Mondays was intense, profound and seemed largely misplaced. Perhaps I was put off by the label's parallel love of the promising but ultimately hapless Stockholm Monsters. I'm sure this tainted my vision of the band in those early days and perhaps coloured any reviews I might write about them. Not that, for one moment, I thought any members of this band would actually read these reviews. Apparently, they did. When I met with Derek Ryder in November 1996, to discuss the content of this book, he surprised me by making this comment:

"The only think that worries me...and I know it worries Shaun and Gary Whelan and all of them, is that you were always against the band. Not that you wrote bad reviews, but rather that you never understood us. Is that fair?"

I thought not. I admitted being a little confused by the erratic nature of the band in the early days but so what? I was just a local hack. I told him that, in my own little way, I had always completely supported the Mondays. He went away happy. That very night, by an astonishing coincidence and for some reason that completely escapes me, *Manchester Evening News* chose to re-run a review I had written in February 1987 about Happy Mondays. It summed up the problems I saw back then in defining the band's qualities:

"Last Saturday I decided to make one last desperate attempt

to come to terms with the truly erratic, somewhat elusive genius of Happy Mondays. That odd band who are getting odder. So I went to The Boardwalk in search of further enlightenment. I went to see a band who are proud to have the legendary John Cale as producer of their debut album, a forthcoming Factory release which is doomed to be unleashed in a ripple of introverted (de)promotion. In a way, Happy Mondays are perfectly suited to the arrogant reserve of Factory. Their music, which moves from good to god-awful and back again, seems to be coated with a soft, padded outer layer. You really have to work hard to enjoy Happy Mondays. It was like that on Saturday. To stand more than thirty feet from the stage was to stand in confusion. Visually, all that could be seen was a motley crew with a lead singer apparently made of superball rubber The music was dulled and introspective. But, three songs later (and ten paces nearer the stage), Happy Mondays were producing the kind of infectious rolling funk which has gained them ecstatic praises in the most esteemed of quarters. Last year's single, and Factory classic 'Freaky Dancin'" became the highlight of the set. The best I've seen them perform the song and surrounded by a set which lacked bite. Typically unfathomable."

Unfathomable? Perhaps. Confusion surrounded the Mondays in those early days. A confusion promoted by the undeniable fact that they were a 'moment' band. Their sets rose or dipped, succeeded or failed, depending on the state of their ever fluctuating camaraderie, or perhaps on what they had taken that evening. To be fair, my memories of that particular Boardwalk gig, where they headlined over an embryonic Inspiral Carpets in front of less than 150 onlookers, was of a frantic, sweaty rugby scrum of a performance, during which the singer and the, er, bongo player, would clasp each other in a tight embrace, rather like two football supporters enjoying a moment of terrace 'ecstacy', or two footballers locked in excessive goal celebrations. And it *was* a celebration too. A celebration of simply having the bottle to get up and have a go. Part of the problem was that it was a private joke.

As a casual on-looker, as a mere 'punter', one didn't quite feel as though you had been invited to the party. However, there was enough charisma bouncing about on that makeshift stage to make the casual observer want to at least join in, to be accepted. But it was a club within a club and, looking back, it would seem that the only membership credentials needed would be to hail from the vicinity of, if not actually in Little Hulton - a strange, coldly evocative collection of council houses and northern terraces, situated between Manchester and Bury. Even then, Happy Mondays were a 'type'. They represented something. They were so obviously a gang. Then there was Bez, the original 'Freaky Dancer'. A mere 'hanger-on' during the New Order support tour, his limpet artlessness would soon become curiously and famously essential. At times, when he wrenched himself away from the clutching on stage bonhomie of Shaun, he would veer off in a rhythmic direction of his own. Not necessarily out of time but just, somehow, on a separate plain. You could wander, tentatively, towards the stage front, as I did one Saturday at The International Club, and simply stare hard into his eyes. What was there? Two blackened dots, staring, stock still, firing a glare at some meaningless point at the rear of the hall. His eyes would be his central pivot, pinning him in place while, all around, his body would seem to be wading through an ocean of treacle. A strange spectacle indeed. Not without charisma. Not without talent either. Having said that, one always felt that the 'Bez's Guide To Classic Maracas Playing' was an unlikely book, indeed.

Freaky Dancin'

The story behind the Mondays introduction to Factory, and vice versa did, in fact, have several strands. Despite being attacked in several music papers for rigging the aforementioned talent contest so the Mondays would win, when in reality they came last, Tony Wilson denies even being there. "I don't recall any talent night at all. I'm told they did play one but that wasn't the night that we all saw the band," he states. In fact, he had been alerted to the idiosyncratic charms of the band by Factory A&R man Mike Pickering who had bumped into Phil Saxe in his native Bramhall. (A plush Stockport suburb where Pickering and his friend Martin Fry had been the first two punks to wander idly through Bramhall's leafy streets). "I kept thinking that Happy Mondays were from St. Helens, I always thought it was St. Helens," Wilson states, "Though that was obviously me getting it wrong. Clearly it was Little Hulton, but it was way after the alleged talent night that I first saw them. We all trouped down to The Hacienda to see them. Me, Rob (Gretton, New Order manager/Factory director) and Alan Erasmus (Factory Director). I remember standing at the bar, watching them and thinking, "Yeah, this is us." It was so obvious, really. Rob liked them, too, which was unusual because Rob never seemed to like anything, so we just knew we would work with them. We weren't phased by their laddishness, either. Remember, we already had The Stockholm Monsters on Factory. They were mad working class bastards from the north of Manchester, who had a bit of funk and a bit of spunk about them. So, in effect, Happy Mondays weren't providing us with anything we didn't already have. Mind you, perhaps we should have seen the signs. We'd had a few nightmares with the Monsters, bless 'em. What I'm saying is that the concept was already in place. The Mondays had a new slant on it but it was, very much, a Factory concept. The kind of band that no other record company in the world would consider touching at any cost. So, obviously, they were perfect for us."

Hanging Around

In 1985, immediately following the band's support spots with New Order, Shaun Ryder managed to meet and befriend fellow Manchester United fanatic, the awesomely sardonic,

Terry Hall. Mainly because of a desire to be situated closer to Old Trafford, but partly to escape the suffocating pressures of insular Coventry, Hall had moved from the Midlands base he had famously occupied since the beginning of The Specials, and had settled in the hugely unlikely Derbyshire village of Hayfield, famous only for an annual jazz festival. In a sense, the isolation suited Hall who openly stated that all he wished to do with his music was to make enough money to be able to "fuck off for good. To the Lake District or somewhere." This somewhat pragmatic approach appealed to Ryder, who shared Hall's loathing of rock's sycophantic fringes. Hall was, like New Order, profoundly anti-star and Ryder fought hard to contain his mild awe. The Fun Boy Three and The Specials had been particular favourites of Ryder's, partly because of their mod-ish connotations and partly because Ryder always displayed curiously eclectic musical tastes. Ryder was also well acquainted with the unassuming ex-Bluebell and future member of The Smiths Craig Gannon, who had startled most of his friends in his Trafford neighbourhood by joining Hall's post Fun Boy three unit, The Colourfield, who were the oddest of bands. Exuberant, sarcastic, mocking and laddish offstage, they could be astonishingly sexist, utterly anti-PC, quite something in the 'right on' days of the mid-eighties. Yet as soon as they took up a position in the spotlight, they would become withdrawn, introverted even. Ryder loved this. He also loved Hall's utterly don't-give-a-fuck stage presence which, in truth, often verged on the unforgivably blasé. Ryder, and the rest of the Mondays, would briefly follow The Colourfield from gig to gig, closely observing the level of professionalism that really did lie behind the apathy.

"All our gigs, up until then had really been one offs," stated Ryder, "and we really didn't know how a band worked. We didn't even know how a band rehearsed, properly, so I once went along to see Colourfield in rehearsal in Liverpool, just to see how it was done. I learnt a lot from Terry. People thought he didn't care how he looked in front of an audience, but that wasn't the case. He worked a crowd really well." Like Barney

Sumner, John Lydon and Mark E Smith, Hall knew how to project arrogance, how to court enigmatic aloofness without looking a prat. Not an easy feat. Ryder simply watched and looked and learned.

Delightful

The band's first single, 'Delightful' was in fact, anything but. Oh, that's not quite fair - listen hard and you will hear, through the muddiness, the joyous clangings of a band determined to have a good time. It was, if nothing else, wholly representative of a half-formed band who lay at the mercy of their producer. Encouragingly it didn't, however, sound quite like all the other half-formed star-struck spotties who were anxious to slap themselves down on vinyl, and in so doing managed only to transfer demo standard dabblings into a format that dulled the effect even further. But there was something more to Happy Mondays than that. Listen hard and something emerges, some kind of vision.

It had been produced by Mike Pickering who, after his years with Quando Quango and, prior to that, Martin Fry's Vice Versa, knew his way around a studio. The Mondays didn't. They fell into the control room like so many star-struck schoolboys, soaking in the glamour, loving the sexiness of the ambience. Pickering, as he later admitted, had his hands full. In truth, the band's attitude was correct. With no intention of turning the entire thing into a chore, let alone a vocation, they merely wanted to find a different angle on the fine art of getting stoned, bladdered and wrecked. Nothing wrong with that - indeed, in time it would profoundly and famously flavour their work. With 'Delightful', it didn't quite manage to download into the recording. It merely dulled the song's brittle edges. There was, initially, a glorious irony about the 'Delightful' single. When Mike Pickering brought the tape back to Factory's office on Palatine Road, Tony Wilson wasn't too impressed. He had to fight hard to conceal his disappointment. "It wasn't how I envisaged them at all," he later states, "in fact, it really was strange because Mike had brought out that indie sound, that's how he saw them, but I had heard something different. Something that was to do with the 'wah wah' guitar sound. That's what had excited me."

Ironic indeed. As if in a reflection of early A Certain Ratio, and the parallels were many, Wilson had seen Happy Mondays as a great new soul hope, soul punk perhaps, a stunning jagged, embryonic funk. He saw them as a dance band, a band who would happily spread across club-bound 12" singles, a band to bounce along to, a working class street dance. Whereas Mike Pickering, a great dance music innovator, one of the most important Hacienda DJ's, and the later driving force of M People - in other words a future stalwart of international dance music - was actually the man who drained the dance-ability straight out of the first Happy Mondays single. Ironic indeed. Perhaps one shouldn't lay too much blame on Pickering's shoulders. After all, he had been confronted with an unruly mob who didn't have a clue what a studio was, what it was for and what could be achieved within it and never showed the slightest attempt to understand it either. The studio was Strawberry. Strawberry without Martin Hannett, who had fallen onto the flipside of Factory, (more later) and not a particularly happy place for Pickering either. His previous band, Quando Quango, had experienced all manner of trauma during a recording session which included a legendary spat with a distinctly unimpressed American producer. Before Pickering, there had been some talk of The Durutti Column's thin, enigmatic guitar genius, Vini Reilly, taking control of the unenviable task. Reilly, who had made an art form of fluctuating between affability and downright irritability, seemed a ludicrous choice but both Saxe and Wilson thought this was an inspired idea (very Factory-esque) and even went as far as dispatching Reilly to Strawberry for an 'experimental session'. Within two hours of working with the Mondays, Vini Reilly had returned to the Factory office, his head held low in his hands in a state of total disbelief.

"I cannot spend another second in their fucking presence," he stated, before ominously adding, "Those people are total scumbags, fucking mental scumbags. No-one should be forced to work with them. They are the worst bastards I have ever come into contact with. Thank you Tony, thanks a fucking lot. And I thought A Certain Ratio were bad!" In truth, Vini had been hit by a barrage of insular Salford banter, probably borne more out of nervousness than arrogance, though it was obviously difficult to tell the difference. But the portents were not all bad. Indeed, Reilly noticed, from within the general cacophony, something genuinely interesting. He continued "That guitarist, you know what Tony, he has absolutely no idea how to play the fucking guitar. He has no idea what he is doing at all. That's the strange thing, because what he actually is doing, or rather, what he is trying to do, is potentially the most inventive stuff that anyone has played for at least ten years." Vini had really hit upon something, but it was most unlike the perceptive Pickering not to notice it also, even more unlike him to stubbornly repress it. But it was obviously there...somewhere...an unusual noise lost in the undertone, screaming to get out. It did not escape on 'Delightful', originally a slow, spacey, almost ambient groove number which had been battered into resembling early Smiths or James (well, everything in Manchester sounded like early Smiths or James in those days). Two other songs surfaced on the 12" only EP. The equally jerked up 'This Feeling' and the intriguingly entitled, 'Oasis'. Only on this track was it possible to sense the future movement of the band. A fact which obviously failed to escape the notice of Happy Mondays themselves, as it would later resurface on their debut album. It is, perhaps, interesting to note that the 'Delightful' EP which slipped out practically unnoticed among a strange little huddle of Factory recordings, appeared in exactly the same month (September 1985) as the ill-fated debut disc by The Stone Roses, the forgettable 'So Young', notable only because of the involvement of producer Martin Hannett.

*   *   *

In truth, the breakthrough years of Happy Mondays would probably have been a mite more positive, had the arguments been allowed to rage a little more fluently. As it was, things were occasionally allowed to fester. Phil Saxe illuminated further: "They had an argument once and decided not to talk to one of the band. He didn't notice for three days, and they were living in the same house. They're a funny bunch. Brilliant, though. I think it might be some kind of private language. There have been times when they would babble on forever, and I haven't had a clue what they were going on about. But they weren't freezing me out, they were just being totally natural. I think it came as a bit of a surprise for them to discover that not everyone could understand their witterings. They came from a small world, in one sense. Small and insular, with its own language." Indeed, that's exactly what it was. A private gang-line flow of communication and non communication into which not even their manager and cohort was allowed to tap. It was, and remains, a Swinton thing.

At the time, Happy Mondays were living in Lower Broughton, a distinctive neighbourhood blessed with a superficial shabbiness. Downbeat, decayed and grubby around the edges but peppered with pubs that still held an atmosphere of 'the local'. Not that they were exactly the Rovers Return - no Mavis Riley ever crossed these thresholds, but they were always simmering with the bubble and chatter of local gossip, all topped, of course, with the faint air of menace they would reserve for the occasional stranger. In a sense, this impenetrable fortress was the true scene which surrounded Happy Mondays. And they were content to remain there, aloof, from many of the 'lesser' bands who would attempt to stimulate a Manchester camaraderie within the practice room complex at The Boardwalk, situated deep in Manchester's Little Peter Street.

The Boardwalk. A dark, dank, Gothic ex-Victorian schoolhouse kicked into shape by geography graduate Colin Sinclair, who transformed it into a dusty venue-cum-rehearsal room for practically all the burgeoning Manchester acts of the day. It went on to become one of the city's most innovative and respected dance venues. In 1985, in The Boardwalk, any aspect of local band gossip could be instantly accessed, usually with hugely entertaining results. The Mondays, being quite the antithesis of the raincoated, student-ish norm, never seemed to quite fit into the prevailing camaraderie. Indeed, it has been stated, though the band would furiously object to this, that Happy Mondays were the band most responsible for breaking the warm, gang-like feel of the building. Paul Ryder: "There are plenty of bands that live here and one or two of them are alright. But there's no such thing as the Manchester scene. It's the worst ones that need to feel part of a movement or a scene. We don't. We're not part of any scene."

The Mondays might have denied its existence, but contrary to latter-day rumour, there *was* an exciting and bewilderingly disparate mid-eighties, pre-Madchester 'scene' in Manchester. It may have been fuelled by a somewhat frantic competitiveness, it may have been split into several cliquish strands. Nevertheless, the run-in to the Madchester explosion had kick started in the summer of 1985, when the tiny Boardwalk, the larger International and the more dance-orientated Hacienda had formed an infamous Manchester gig triangle. Local bands played a variety of gigs from small headline spots at The Boardwalk, to medium sized supports at the larger venues, and back again, going round and round in circles. In the wake of The Smiths (who seemed invincible at the time), New Order, Simply Red, Carmel, The Fall and The Chameleons, came a whole flood of breaking bands. Happy Mondays and The Stone Roses were sitting alongside the weird, wired folk of James, the daft polemics of Rough Trade-signed Easterhouse, jazzers Kalima, pretty boy hip poppers The Railway Children, scruff punksters The Membranes, noisy Hulme industrialists Tools You Can Trust, poppy Glossopians The Bodines, psychedelic garage band Inspiral Carpets, Johnny Dangerously's Ignition, Marc Riley's Creepers, Andrew Berry's Weeds....on and on and on. All serviced by a swamp of well-read local media. Hip young listings mag *City Life*, smart sober

Hulme fanzine *Debris*, glossy popzine *Muze*, 'The Word' page in *The Manchester Evening News*, Dave Haslam and Sarah Champion in *NME*, Tony 'The Greek' Michaelides on Piccadilly Radio. It all seemed, somehow, confined, constrained, exciting and home-grown. Yes, there was a Manchester scene. The best local scene, in fact, since the demise of the post-punk industrialists in the late seventies.

Happy Mondays played the scene as effectively as anyone else, with Phil Saxe repeatedly slapping their first two singles, 'Delightful' and 'Freaky Dancin'' on every influential desk in the north west. It was working for them too although, it must be remembered, Happy Mondays lay some way off the pace, fitting somewhere between Easterhouse and soon-to-be Creation signings The Bodines. Despite this, like all great bands, they would still cling resolutely to their treasured aloofness. Shaun Ryder: "There's them, like...an' then there's fucking us. I'm not saying that we are any better but, like, a lot of bands seem to be in some kind of muso's fucking club, right. But we don't fucking like that, 'cos we aren't muso's. We aren't anything like that. We hang around with our mates, we are just like them and they're all we'll ever need. I'm not saying we aren't flash gits and want to get on, but that's the point. I tell you what, we can't be smug 'cos we ain't got a fuckin' penny between us an' some of the lads who have started to follow us are dressed in dead smart gear an' that. I'm always thinking, "Fuck me, I wish I could afford that." So we sell 'em some stuff, yer know, going in clubs with loads of stuff in little packets. We are just drug dealers who happen to be in a band rather than the other way around. None of the other bands can fuckin' say that, can they? But if we ever do make it, like New Order, there will still be us an' the gang around us. I know everyone says that, but that's how it is with us, and it always will be."

Aloof they may have been, but they still felt an affinity to Factory. Gary Whelan: "I'd rather be on Factory than any other independent label," and, a touch sarcastically, "It's like one big happy family, but we would move down to London if the money was right." The whole band agreed with this sentiment. Phil Saxe: "It's about making money and securing a job. Because otherwise Happy Mondays are on the dole." The "one big, happy family" status of Factory was thus a rather precarious affair. And it was an affair that nearly cracked in mid-1986 when, following a spell of Factory despondency, Rough Trade's Geoff Travis came within a whisker of signing the band and tempting them away behind Factory's back. Nothing wrong with that. Factory's only contract was concealed, at the time, within the sentence, "All our bands have freedom, the freedom to fuck off." Behind the back of the band, Phil Saxe had been talking as well. Travis: "I recall being utterly convinced at one point that we had got the Mondays, although I'm not sure quite when it was. I always knew that they had something special, right back from hearing their first singles, and I wanted them. Mind you, I was equally convinced about Easterhouse who looked like becoming the next U2 but you never know. But yes, we were all set up for Happy Mondays. That would have been fun. Thinking back, Factory did a great job with them." Things might have swung a little in Rough Trade's favour had the piece of paper that languished somewhere deep in a dusty file at Factory's office, supporting the words, "Our artists own all the music and we own nothing" been more readily available.

Despite this uncertainty, and Saxe's open-minded approach, there was a fairly solid strand of friendship running between Factory and the band, A strand that was fixed, most firmly, with New Order. Ever since the tour of '85, during which the Mondays had been amazed to find themselves treated so well, this bond had remained in place. There was also New Order's Barney Sumner, whose often rather cruelly under-rated production skills had been used on the Mondays second single 'Freaky Dancin'/The Egg.' Working with Barney was dead easy, as Shaun Ryder told *NME*'s Dave Haslam: "He was on the same wavelength. He knew what he wanted and he never rushed anything." Under-rated is stating it rather mildly, as Tony Wilson would say to this writer "Barney was one of the finest producers ever to come out of Manchester, all those great singles that you didn't know he produced...The Monday's 'Freaky Dancin'', pure Barney, that one. Section 25's 'Looking From A Hilltop', loads of classic stuff. All Barney with perhaps just a little input from Donald." (Johnson, drummer for A Certain Ratio).

Sumner succeeded where Pickering had curiously though understandably failed. With 'Freaky Dancin'' and 'The Egg' began that strange, infectious, eery, creeping, spine-tingling rhythm. The 'sway' of The Mondays. A sound that was almost like a lot of other sounds - *almost but not quite*. Barney managed, at least in part, to capture the feel that Wilson had sensed and perhaps this is the true measure of a great producer - potentially better than Hannett. Barney always shielded himself and his considerable intelligence, with an aura of rather childish detachment. But out of this scary liaison came 'Freaky Dancin'', most definitely the beginning of something. No-one recognised it at the time, but it was the beginning of something that would become bigger than the band. While The Stone Roses were still shedding their juvenile goth skin, good songs were beginning to appear - Happy Mondays had stumbled into a formula. A layered 'wah wah' guitar sound placed skillfully over a heavy backbeat. The embryonic stirrings of the Happy Mondays' celebrated 12" sound, backed by the soon-to-be-legendary 'The Egg', which cast a strange nod towards Pete Wylie's Wah Heat, especially with Ryder's arrogant vocal drawl.

'Freaky Dancin'' was also the beginning of something else. It was the beginning of Bez. No longer just a spaced out mate who would hang around, humping equipment, lolloping around the studio and the dressing room. It occurred to the band that Bez was part and parcel of this gang. More than that, he was strangely inspiring, bizarrely enigmatic. The band began to realise that his presence on stage might make the visuals - sadly dour until this point - a little more exciting. He couldn't dance but he looked interesting. Bez didn't so much 'join' the Mondays, he simply evolved into a part of them. Like an extra limb. It wasn't always apparent quite what he did but, before long, when Bez wasn't there, something was missing. If nothing else, he provided an extra (and by all accounts incredibly astute) pair of ears. For a band like Happy Mondays, eight parts influence, one part inspiration, one part perspiration, all tied together with such a loose knot of musicianship, a 'sussed' extra sense was a valuable asset.

One might reasonably expect that given serious, if not financially powered, commitment from Factory, the band would spend their days locked in their rehearsal rooms, playing, writing, experimenting and frequently surfacing to perform at small venues across the country. But again, this was not an average gang of eager beaver rock hopefuls, only too grateful to be granted the opportunity to lunge about on deadening support spots. But it wasn't the band who were beginning to gain momentum, it was the speed of their constantly swirling state of party.

"To be honest," Ryder would claim, "although I did always want to live a rock 'n' roll life, it wasn't really the music I craved. Other people got much more excited about that than me. It was a means to get into a lifestyle, an' it came via me Dad. I was right into sex, drugs and rock 'n' roll, but the rock 'n' roll part always seemed like the weakest part of those three. It was a way of getting more of the other two." Contrary to popular rumour, Shaun Ryder and cohorts did not spend the early months of 1986 prowling the Hacienda dance floor. This would have been difficult as, by this time, their party had extended across the world, with Manchester little more than a occasional meeting point. Much of the time they spent in Amsterdam or, as it is still affectionately known, 'The Dam'. This was the period and the place where E became a stable part of the Shaun Ryder diet.: 1986 was an important time, "he later informed *Arena*, "I fucked off to the Dam for about a year and grew me hair. I had my first E in the Dam. It was one of them real tiny, dead good Doves. I felt really great, dead happy and I had this thing about being clean, all shaved and all that lot. Got rid of the fucking goatee. And I didn't want to drink beer. I had Perrier water and I didn't really feel anything, all I knew was that I felt fantastic. Then I kind of learnt the buzz."

Shaun Ryder and friends have claimed, in *Arena*, in *The Face* and in several late eighties rave fanzines, that they were largely responsible for introducing the drug ecstacy, 'E' onto the Manchester dance floors during the mid-to-late eighties. (Although to Ryder's credit, he would later state in the November 1996 issue of *Arena* that, "I must stress that (taking 'E') wasn't the right thing to do") These 'claims' are founded in the curious period which followed the release of 'Delightful', and the insertion of Bez as percussionist and dancer.

Mondays cohort, self-confessed bootlegger and ligger, Charlie, recalls this period: "It was the wildest of times. I mean, it wasn't just Amsterdam and it wasn't just 1986. A gang of, let's say, Mondays people, sort of evolved during the years before that. Some of us were into pirating. Printing up posters and T-shirts of bands who were touring Europe and we'd pile into a van and just take off. Throughout the early eighties really, a whole network of faces from Salford and Wythenshaw began to spring up..You'd see these people all over the place. You'd go in to some stupid little bar, in some god-forsaken village in Spain or somewhere and you'd find Bez asleep in the fucking corner. Or you'd see some van speeding along a really dangerous mountainside road and you'd know...that's a Salford van. We got everywhere and the Mondays thing was a big part of that. I'd say that the Mondays grew out of that weird, loose scene rather than the other way around. I'd always known Shaun and I remember those Amsterdam days really well. We'd just be bouncing from coffee bar to coffee bar, totally in a dream, but not just for a weekend - it was for months on end. You know that joke about Bez living in a cave in Morocco, well, it's fucking true, he did. I don't know whether this has happened before but, suddenly there was a whole lot of Salford and Manchester lads, none of whom ever had any money and most were on the dole, who would exist on a worldwide scale. Really odd. You'd see some cunt staggering down a dusty Spanish lane in the middle of fucking nowhere on Monday...and then you'd see the same person turning up at the dole office on Thursday. How did they do it? Just jibbing, blagging, scrounging. It was street logic. It wasn't just the Mondays, it was far bigger than that really, but they were the first band to grow out of such a scene. At least, as far as I'm aware."

CHAPTER 5

Cale And Able

In looking for a producer for the first Mondays album, Tony
Wilson was drawn to his record collection for inspiration.
Cambridge-educated Wilson was struck by how such an ill-
educated man as Ryder could write with such originality,
vision and individual perception, and he was reminded of the
similar clarity he had found upon first hearing Patti Smith's
Horses back in the mid-seventies. Alongside The Ramones,
Smith carved the first few notches into the ideal that became
punk, lifting lyric above music, casting her poetic eye across
the US landscape and culture whilst retaining a personal grasp
on the listener, such that the album is still considered a
genuine classic some twenty years later.

Horses was produced by John Cale, ex-Velvet Underground,
master of the avant garde, and a unique character in the
contemporary rock field through the sixties, seventies and
eighties. He still retains a reputation for finding alternative
routes in the musical process, channelling energies in unusual
directions to get the best out of both his own work and that he
produces. Wilson, planning for his brand new Mondays
album, saw John Cale as the ideal character to make a classic
out of their raw, perhaps otherwise unworkable debut album.

Wilson's idea to use Cale as producer wasn't a mere
gimmick. There were solid reasons for it. Some of them,
contrary to the Factory norm, had the flavour of advanced
marketing. It was always unlikely to be a big seller, whatever
the future might hold for the band, but with Cale at the
controls it would always hold a certain curiosity value for a
small stream of trainspotter fanatics who would keep sales
ticking over into the foreseeable future. No big deal, perhaps,
but even if everything fell flat, it would be enough to whittle
away stocks over a considerable time. For once, Factory were

acting very much like the major labels who, in those days, always linked an unsigned band with a notable producer. It was contractual, an insurance policy but one that saw so many bands aligned with producers for reasons that would never be discovered. Maybe it was different with the Mondays and Cale, for it was hard to see a major label allowing such an unsettling, and perhaps disturbing record to be made in the first place.

Wilson only made it to the recording sessions on one occasion and, even then, he only managed to see Cale for about five minutes. "I regret that, now," he admits, "in fact, in a way, I regret the whole John Cale thing. To be honest, he didn't have a fucking clue what was going on. He'd never met anyone like the Mondays before, he had no idea what the fuck they were going on about, or what they were trying to achieve, or why, or how far it might go, or anything. It must have been pretty terrible for him. Imagine being holed up in Stockport with these crazed locals. In retrospect, I don't think the album worked. Oh, maybe it did, on one level, but it could have been so much better."

Squirrel And G-Man Twenty Four Hour Party People Plastic Face Carnt Smile, (White Out) always remained deliberately uncomfortable. One recalls the day it began to scream from the record racks - a loud, brash, art-lessly vivid sleeve, quite the antithesis of Factory's low key tradition. Far from emitting the image that (in the Factory way) lay just over the horizon, forcing the fans to reach out a little, this was a profoundly 'in-yer-face' affair. This record was the vinyl equivalent of the gang of lads who invade your serenity on an Inter City train. They gather around you, a mess of in-jokes and crude quibbling, ripping open endless cans of beer, becoming increasingly boisterous, more than mildly threatening. You shuffle in your seat and attempt to bury yourself in your book. You fail miserably to emit an aura of detachment and your efforts, sadly, seem only to spur them on. Eventually you are faced with a choice. Either you slink away in defeat and find another seat or you rip open a beer, and join the party. For a long while, the hip, young music buyers of Manchester remained torn between these two extremes. Tune in or tune out. The Mondays were up and dancing. This was a record that didn't sit well in most record collections and, once on the turntable, proved absolutely impossible to ignore. Far from masking the considerable inadequacies of Ryder's voice (which would have been the initial goal of most producers), Cale chose to courageously enhance them. To lift the voice until it hovered precariously apart and aloft from the loose funk tangle below. And what a tangle it was. A thousand nights, drunk on funk, dull thuds and a wandering bass, a wholly intoxicated and, if the mood fitted, intoxicating sound. It was easy to dismiss the overall effect as an inarticulate muddle - as many did - but then it soon began to dawn on the listener that there was more going on here than just another gang of mouthy but inept pseudo-musos gathered in by a clever producer. This was the previously ignored sound of Salford soul demanding a slice of the action. The vocals, unfathomable to most who lived more than three miles from Ryder's house as well as most who lived within it, proved to be circles of curiously tight word-plays. It was the kind of young Salford dialect that would tax John Cooper Clarke, let alone a potential record buyer in Seattle, but poetic nonetheless. It dawned on many that Shaun Ryder was, in fact, a talent fighting to escape his circumstances and his musical shortcomings. He needn't have worried. His 'non-vocals' were in excellent company, as Dylan, Reed, Shelley, Sumner etc. etc. would surely testify.

The album's title has, as intended, caused a thousand journalists to fall into a pitiful state of fruitless investigation What could it mean, this lovely, ugly, evocative and rather poetic bundle of words? Well, you'd have to be Shaun Ryder to fully understand, and even then I'm not so sure. 'Squirrel' was the nickname of Knobhead's mother, apparently according to the band because "she looks like a squirrel". 'G-Man' was a reference to Bez's Dad, simply because he was a cop. 'Twenty Four Hour Party People' could very easily have been the name of the band. It was how they were often described, and how they described themselves. Ryder: "It was like a title for whizz freaks, which we were...amongst other things." 'Plastic Face' and 'Carnt Smile' were just two truncated Salford expressions, both relating to "miserable bastards." Shaun Ryder: "I put all these words together, initially just as a joke, messin' about but, well, I thought it sounded pretty neat. Kind of summed the whole thing up. I remember telling the rest of the band and they just fell about. They thought I was completely mad and just said, "No way, no way, you'll ruin us. For a while I thought they were right but everyone sort of grew to like it."

As strongly hinted by Wilson, the band's relationship with Cale had been vague. Shaun was the only band member fully aware of Cale's heady repertoire of dark, keyboard-orientated subterranean pop albums. A mass of rather surprisingly buoyant songs all hiding a black side, enhanced by Cale's unsettling and enigmatic voice. Cale's pre-Velvet's background was of a distinctly non-rock 'n' roll nature. Indeed his schooling in classical and avant garde has often been regarded as the most dominating, refreshing aspect of the Velvet's sound, effectively distancing them from their peers. Throughout Cale's post-Velvet's work, that same distance had been maintained, keeping his music firmly away from the mainstream, yet intriguingly idiosyncratic.

Cale had never attempted to make any secret of his various chemical addictions, so he was more than able to come to terms with the excesses of this young band. Simply, massively and famously, he'd 'been there'. Although he latterly kept his habits at bay - and his weight down - by consuming huge quantities of fruit, he was always able to understand the ups and downs of the various band members. He exploited their most productive artistic moments, although it didn't always work out that way. Shaun Ryder: "A lot of people have since told me how great they thought that first album was. To be totally honest, I always thought it was shite, all of it. In them days I didn't really give a toss. It was hardly a professional attitude. I just wanted some quick money. I didn't want to spend weeks in some studio grafting away, fuck that. The music didn't matter to me at all, really. It was just us lot having a good time. A big game. Cale was okay but he got on me nerves a bit, he kept wanting us to work an' that."

The madness, of course, wasn't just restricted to the music. What often passed for Salford street slang, that great mass of bewildering words and non-words that were scattered across the album and continued the nonsense of the title, wasn't actually from Salford. It wasn't even Little Hulton, Swinton school yard or Lower Broughton tap room slang. Or even Mondays-speak. It was a pure stream of Ryder-esque consciousness: "Pure fucking stupid drivel" said Shaun. "Pure genius" maintains Tony Wilson to this day. "It is one of my ambitions to gather together all Shaun's lyrics and put them out in a book. I regard him as one of Salford's greatest poets. People laugh, but I really do. As a Cambridge graduate, I regard him like Yeats. I think he is certainly the best lyric writer since Dylan."

It has to be said that some of it didn't prove too difficult to work out. One thinks, for instance, of Shaun Ryder picking up a porno book back in the early eighties, as he was undoubtedly prone to do. Within the pages he discovered a headline 'Mad Fuck Film Story'. He liked the sound of 'Mad Fuck'. Immediately, it was stored away in the darkest recesses of his mind, from where, six years later, he would retrieve it, turn it around and use the words as a song title. 'Kuff Dam'. Simple and effective enough to keep journalists guessing for several months. Paul Ryder, leaping cryptically onto the tale, would later accuse Shaun. "You didn't know what that really meant until ya' started visiting a maternity clinic, didya?"

Strange

Shaun Ryder: "We never write songs as such. Lyrics just come out of me 'ead. Most of 'em are just words strung together like. They just fit. Just childish rhymes. Like this mate of mine who used to go in the chippy and ask for "rabbit dropping pooh pooh pooh cacky plop" for his dinner. The woman would have to guess what he wanted. That's our brain. That's how it always has been. There's a lot of words in our songs that have got fuck all to do with the songs. Ever listened to Abba? Abba couldn't speak English when they wrote those songs, could they? Like me. I don't really want to make sense myself. I couldn't write a song that was about something. I'm not that clever. I'm a rapper, whatever. I admire people with a few brains though. I wish I had brains, could have been a brain surgeon." He continues "Most of the songs are put together like short stories from the Twighlight Zone. They are not about anything real. Little black comedies. I'm quite happy singing about something meaningless as long as it's witty. You put your own pictures to it."

That's Shaun Ryder. Not as dumb as he would have us believe. Not as sneakily evasive, either. Like many of the most intriguing rock stars, and certainly like most Manchester bands, Ryder's inspiration came from a gigantic, space-crushing record collection. And, right there, in those last few sentences, as he talked about his 'songwriting technique', you can just picture him squatting on the floor to the sounds of Captain Beefheart, to Zappa, to Bowie and, most of all, to his fellow Salfordian, Mark E Smith. Indeed, the missing link between The Fall and The Fatback Band. It would be easy to place Smith on a higher intellectual plain, but, in effect, his art is similar to Ryder's. Everyday surreal observations, scruffily slammed down into a pocket book, onto the back of a beer mat, twisted around, mixed up, messed up, forgotten about, rediscovered, placed alongside something totally different. New meaning appears. The art of writing oblique pop lyrics. A natural process but not as simple as it may seem. It takes a talent, a talent that one senses even Shaun Ryder can't begin to understand. "Like when I was in this bar abroad," he once stated, "this geezer walked past me and said, "Shift." He just wanted me out of the way. He thought that was the word. He meant "Excuse me, mate." There'd have been no point in him coming up to me and sayin' "Semi detached House". I wouldn't have understood him. Our songs are like that, in a way. They are a mistake. A mis-use of words. Something that is not quite right. Something and nothing." Something and nothing? Perhaps something that had escaped before education managed to close it down? There is something hugely romantic about a talent that totally escapes the clutches of the educational system. The true essence, perhaps, of a rock 'n' roll success story.

*   *   *

The pre-album single 'Tart Tart' was partly about, as the Mondays might say, "a bird". It was a girl called Dinah who felt sorry for Shaun and Bez's ragamuffin looks and lowly status, often providing them with a roof over their heads when they'd arrive back in Salford, doped, bladdered, stunned, silent and cold. She was one of the few people they had met who understood them. She wasn't an angel - indeed, she would earn a crust by peddling drugs - but she was one of the first people to take this strange and dubious twosome at all seriously. Tragically, Dinah would later die of a brain haemorrhage. The song was about other, darkly related, things too. Inside 'Tart Tart' you might discover a splattering of references to Factory/Mondays producer Martin Hannett, even though Ryder was yet to meet him. This baffled a good many people, including Wilson, who could never quite understand just how Ryder had managed to pin down Hannett's character in such a few, short, sharp words. The answer was simple. Since the recording of 'Freaky Dancin'', Ryder had been spending many hours in the company of Barney Sumner, down the Hac, standing at the bar of The International. All this time he would listen agog, to the tales of Martin Hannett, this strange, wildly erratic creature, both blighted and inspired by hedonism, capable of fantastic surges of sheer creativity and before falling back into a wholly negative mess. Ryder loved the very idea of Hannett. The awkwardness, the very real danger that his story might (as indeed it did) end in tragedy at any second. The blind alleys, the mistakes, Hannett on the edge. Hear this in 'Tart Tart'. An edgy song from the fringe and, perhaps, the first recorded sign that Happy Mondays, for better or worse, were very much the real thing.

The remainder of Ryder's subject matter, especially on that first album, became notoriously ambiguous, impenetrable even. You would have to be a member of the band, for example, to know that the second to last track 'Russell' was simply lifted wholesale from a postcard sent to the band from their new found friends and label-mates, A Certain Ratio. The front of the card featured a photograph of Russell Grant. Was that the faint stirring of a Factory clique? Of Mondays elitism? Or was it just something that Shaun Ryder happened to have to hand when he needed a handy lyric? One strongly suspects the latter. Arguably the most critically celebrated track on the album was probably the drippy, melodic slush which regaled in the fitting title 'Olive Oil'. A lovely soft groove. For what's it worth, I don't think I'll every forget the first time I heard the hard slab funk of 'Kuff Dam' or 'Little Matchstick Owen', reworked from the flipside of 'Tart Tart'.

Despite the heady expectations of the Factory team, the album sold poorly. A brief surge in sales followed a sniff of publicity which surrounded the Mondays' sampling of The Beatles. The track 'Desmond', borrowed samples - and a great deal more - from The Beatles song 'Obla Di Obla Da'. Factory reluctantly promised that the first 3,000 pressings, which included this sample, would be destroyed and with this dubious promise appeared to satisfy everyone concerned. Of course, Factory lied through their teeth. As it happened, not one Happy Mondays album fell into the furnace. Despite milking this little legal squabble for every possible millimetre of press, the album still refused to sell. Factory pressed 10,000 and, with the help of considerable push from a smattering of journalists, expected most of them to sell through fairly quickly. Alas, only 3,500 copies of the album were sold during the first six months and, not for the first or last time in Factory's history, an embarrassing pile of records remained unsold in the warehouse. Factory had a history of producing critically acclaimed 'classics' that failed to translate into hard cash - Joy Division's ground-breaking single 'Transmission' being the most notable. It was a hard lesson that the label seemed unable to learn.

"That first Mondays album? Well, it was like flogging a dead horse," says Wilson. "But we loved them and we were committed. It was a typical Factory situation. Today, I always tell my new bands that they will succeed because I now know that great bands always break through, somehow. It's weird but it always happens. But back then, I still wasn't so sure. We'd been pushing The Monsters for so long, and that didn't happen because a lot of things were wrong. But the Mondays, I knew, were a great band. I'd sit down with Shaun and we'd smoke a bit, and he'd be wittering on like some kid out of borstal, completely out of his skull and, somehow I knew he was something special. You could just feel it, he had wonderful charisma. Completely, utterly natural. I knew it would come through in the press, and back then we could get a few good words or a few bad words, all of which helped, but getting the public to wander in and buy the damn thing...it was just impossible."

Alongside the recording and release of the *Squirrel* album, (January to May 1987), the Hacienda's hugely innovative DJ, the aforementioned Mike Pickering, stuffed the club's atmosphere with more and more 'House'. This was particularly evident during the regular Friday night 'Nude Night', so called because there would be "nothing on". Back in the early eighties when Pickering started this, the notion that a DJ could become the magnetic driving force behind a venue (especially a venue that had been purpose-designed as a gig venue), seemed curiously bizarre.

Through a cocktail of soul, rap, salsa, jazz and house, Pickering noticed that he had started to attract a wholly different kind of audience. Not the usual overcoated students at all, but the previously celebrated Perry Boys: casuals, scallies and, most unexpectedly, the new crowd was about sixty percent black. This astonished and delighted Pickering, whose eclectic dance tastes had always seemed beyond the scope of a Manchester dance floor (it seems odd to write such a line now, but for so many years Manchester was a dance floor backwater). On Nude Nights, Happy Mondays would sneak away from the studio or practice room and soak in Pickering's new collection of sounds. For the band, this proved both inspiring and hugely frustrating, for the gulf between the sounds in their heads, and the sounds they made as a band seemed to be impossible to bridge. It was one thing to stand in a stoned huddle, passing super-hip comments around and using them like currency, but any old northern soulie could do that. But transposing this knowledge into something that can be sold to others seemed impossible. Shaun Ryder would later refer to this gulf by stating, "It's like when you see something and you come to try to draw it on a piece of paper, you can't get it down. It was the same thing with our music. We knew what we wanted it to feel like but we were just learning on the early stuff and we just couldn't get it down. I haven't listened to *Squirrel* for years. All I remember is that there were a lot of spaces, we were trying to do a Doors type of groove but make it dance music as well. The stuff may sound like indie rock now, but at the time indie rock was tighter, faster, winkle-pickered finger and we were putting out spacious things."

In short...funk! The very beauty of *Squirrel* was completely down to that naiveté, to the fact that this was a band straining to reach something way out of their league. It gave the album, and not just 'Tart Tart', an edge - and all first album's should have a strong sense of edge.

CHAPTER 6

"I've never bought a music paper, I don't watch Top Of The Pops, don't listen to radio, hate comedians and bad food. We're not some middle-class graduate band who are into engineering and all that."

Paul Ryder

A couple of years before 1987, the *NME* had insinuated that Factory was a greying dulled mess of ageing hicks and hacks, in a review that climaxed with the words, "Will someone please shut the fucking place up?" By May 1987, it seemed anything but this, a label capable of reaching to the very heart of Manchester's youthful surges and offering numerous tasty and unexpected off-shoots. (It also, let it be said, offered a number of no-hopers - The Royal Family and The Poor, anyone? Blurt, Shark Vegas, The Wake, The Duke Quartet, Thick Pigeon?) Without exactly surging on to a new commercial plateau, the Factory roster in 1987 had attained a young, fresh vibrant feel. The Railway Children, neatly managed by The Boardwalk's Colin Sinclair, looked certain to crack into the mainstream in a big way. The unpredictable left-field pop angle was nicely covered by Miaow, the band created and fronted by *NME* and ex-*City Fun* writer Cath Carroll.

It looked good but, as is so often the case, envy simmered beneath the surface, as hinted by the Mondays' Mark Day in the *NME*: "Other bands on the label go on and on about money, but we can't slag Factory off 'cos they've been good to us. No-one else would encourage us. They got us onto vinyl before we had an inkling what that meant." Shaun: "We are not trailing about in the shadow of New Order, 'cos we go out with them. We get food, booze and treated right. All the time. Other bands moan, but not us. We won't fucking look a gift horse in the mouth, mate. I mean, who else would have us lot? No-one, right?"

True enough. One recalls a Monday's Tuesday night sojourn

to the International Club where various members of the band fell about the bar area and lolloped over the seating at the back of the hall. Their somewhat irritating antics were rather touchingly patrolled by New Order's Peter Hook who picked them up (literally) and dragged them out to a waiting taxi as the evening drew to a close.

Shaun Ryder. "The fact is though, that we all began to get this big reputation as being a daft bunch of cunts around town after that first album, as if it was all part of an act. But it wasn't a fucking act at all, man. It was no different from what we were doing before, but suddenly people would start to recognise us. And that was a right fucking pain in the arse 'cos we still had no money. We were going out selling draw and, being in the band wasn't helping us at all. I never knew it would be like that. To be in the *NME* and *Sounds* all the time - I thought that meant that loads of money would come in. But it meant absolutely fuck all. So we still had to survive, man. But there were a couple of times when, getting bigger, you know, making it, really did seem to sneak through. S'pose, underneath it all, we enjoyed being recognised. We wanted fame, course we fucking did."

Sneaking Through...getting bigger...making it!

In Glasgow, the Mondays were in their usual state - dazed and half drugged, disorientated, dislocated and noisy - as they climbed in the obligatory Ford Transit, dreaming of better days, on the brink, they believed, of genuine stardom. As most successful, and all non-successful bands will testify, the brink of success is an extremely dangerous place to be. It is possible, for instance, not only to see the fruits of success, but to be able to taste them albeit only too fleetingly. The Mondays, of course, had been around rock stars since their inception which in a sense only made matters worse. The barrier between 'happening' and 'not happening' becomes rather blurred from close up, and once crossed carries no guarantee that the band will not zip straight back on to the wrong side. This was how the band found themselves, as they drifted into Glasgow in the van driven by Derek Ryder. A few recent, big music press interviews had certainly added numbers to their audiences, and their notoriety travelled before them, guaranteeing blanket local press coverage before they arrived. Having said that, they couldn't be sure if they were actually getting big or whether this was just an enjoyable but fleeting surge.

That night, turning into Sauciehall Street, a sight greeted them that caused their hearts to pound. Right there, before their very eyes, was a queue. Not a small queue either, but a sizeable four deep corridor of people, snaking around the corner. It was a mass of be-denimed couples, scruffy students and, strangely, scores of frighteningly young looking girls. Shaun Ryder, for one, began to rub his hands with glee, with a "Fucking hell maan, this is gonna be smart" look freezing in his eyes. Until, that is, they reached the front of the queue, and noticed it snaking into the Apollo with the glittering words *"Tonight - On Stage - Wet Wet Wet"* screaming from above the foyer. Twenty yards further down the road, the Mondays, by this time sinking fast into a mass depression, encountered the deserted entrance to the club in which they would later be performing. It was a classic Bad News style rock 'n' roll anticlimax. Fortunately, events were lightened somewhat by the gig itself which, not only seemed to have an extra zip, but was performed before a crowd bolstered by excitable Wet Wet Wet fans who wished to extend their evenings entertainment. Happy Mondays were not yet stars, but during that evening they made quite a few more friends.

Bummed, 1988

At the start of 1988, Phil Saxe was in considerable torment. His 'discovery' of Happy Mondays was a considerable coup - blessed with great A&R ears, Saxe would be the first on the scene of a number of other embryonic young bands - he would later attempt, and hilariously fail, to get Factory to sign both Oasis and Pulp. His skill in nurturing and moulding the chaotic shambles of the early Mondays deserves weighty applause indeed. Without Phil Saxe, god knows what would have happened to the individual members in the wake of the volcanic arguments which would surely have riddled the recording of the first album (in the unlikely event of the band even making it that far). Despite all this, it was Saxe who, to his ultimate credit, realised that if Happy Mondays were to stay together, they would need a manager who actively encouraged their state of party. Who could live in it, be it, love it and survive it. In other words, some kind of nutter.

All of which was fine, for Saxe, for a while, for a year or two, even. However, managing a band like Happy Mondays isn't merely a question of hassling for a few gigs, bugging the record company while sitting back waiting for a share of the royalties. To manage Happy Mondays was to become a member of the gang...lock, stock and barrel. To become a member of the gang was to leap on to the rollercoaster and forsake all other duties. It had to be that way of life thing. But Phil Saxe wasn't a ragamuffin scally with a 100% pure hedonistic bent. Phil Saxe was, first and foremost, a businessman with a business to run. A difficult thing to do, when your band is Happy Mondays, a band on the brink (he was sure) of breaking, big time. A band about to embark on one hell of an international adventure. The manager of Happy Mondays would have to be there, with them, going down the dives, being banged up in the police cells, ringing lawyers, laughing in the face of fearful authority, disregarding bureaucracy in a most un-managerial way. With regret, Saxe decided that it just couldn't be him. There was no way he could afford to launch into full time management of the band. He decided to leave but not before suggesting an appropriately unsuitable fun-time replacement. A man who was fully capable and fully qualified to climb on that most awesome rollercoaster. Nathan McGough.

Nathan McGough was a scouse motormouth who had flitted

around the scene since the early eighties, managing little acts here and there. He was well known to Factory, partly for being a member of The Royal Family and The Poor, as well as for managing their hip young, mid-eighties jazz act Kalima. For a while, he appeared to be the only young manager on the scene who really knew what he was doing. "Nathan is really a stage manager," explained Boardwalk owner Colin Sinclair in 1985, as a sundry collection of Manc acts, topped by the then-breaking (and believe it or not, rather hip) Simply Red, assembled to perform a ground-breaking free festival for International Youth Year, at Manchester's Platt Fields.

Nathan always strangely discouraged any comparisons to, or mentions of, his famous father, the wry Liverpool beat poet Roger McGough O.B.E. Instead, he settled in Manchester, determined to create an impact of his own. For a while he joined forces with DJ and writer Dave Haslam, to form the uncompromising indie label Playhard, which had evolved out of the flexi-disc's sellotaped to Haslam's long lamented fanzine *Debris* (Inspiral Carpets made their vinyl debut in this worthy little format). As Play Hard, Haslam and McGough adopted a credibility-oozing Mark E Smith approach, never once allowing their artists to loose sight of their initial aesthetic leanings. Proudly, they caught bands in that exciting though, more often than not, wholly disorganised early form and thus provided serious competition to Factory. By comparison, and despite their new found freshness, Factory still seemed to have become rather fat and cumbersome. Armed with a violently disparate roster ranging from the violin-led street cacophony of the King Of The Slums to Moss Side street rapper MC Buzz B, Play Hard represented the cutting edge of south Manchester's infamous Bohemia.

However, the ferociously ambitious McGough would never be happy settling into the mundane indie dream, bringing low art to the attention of a few hundred - he always felt in a bigger league. With his hedonistic leanings and a locally legendary lack of tact, added to his increasingly volatile relationship with Factory Records, he seemed to be the perfect choice to take over the managerial reigns of Happy Mondays. More importantly, of course, and after no small number of drug-fuelled forays into the heart of Manchester's clubland with a variety of wildly anarchic meetings, Happy Mondays decided that they liked Nathan McGough. And Factory, quite accustomed to creating rods for their own back, seemed more than happy with the new partnership. Despite this, Nathan's initial task was to break the Factory tradition of no contracts..."all our bands have freedom, the freedom to fuck off."He immediately managed to get the band legally signed to the label. Within a very short time indeed, Nathan had succeeded in prizing real money from Wilson, getting real signatures on paper and, it seemed, carving out a real commitment rather than matey intent - Ryder summed up this scenario and the band's absurd and highly parodic relationship with Factory in this gloriously succinct manner: "Tony Wilson is a shit...a wanker...he wants me dead...he must have thought we'd do a runner or he wouldn't have offered us all that money.....and the fact is, we probably would have pissed off, as well."

CHAPTER 7

"I do know that by the time Bummed came out, I had already knocked down my consumption of E. When we did that album, I could still eat three E's a day, but we were a lot calmer than before."

Shaun Ryder

The word in London was that the Mondays were impossible to produce. Factory recognised that following the John Cale experience, they needed someone for Ryder and Co. who would define their sound once and for all. Critical response to the production of the first album was poor, and sales were disappointing. Whether Cale's involvement was an inspiration or a mistake mattered little. Someone needed to nail the Mondays on tape soon if they were to be rid of the myth of being beyond the skills of any production team.

"Impossible to contain, maybe," admitted Wilson, "but surely not impossible to produce. Cale didn't handle it but then again, it would have to be someone who could go with the flow. To become part of them." In retrospect, the answer to that particular riddle does seem strikingly obvious. However, when Nathan McGough and Factory director Alan Erasmus finally plucked out the name of the man they would pursue, a deathly hush fell over the rest of the Factory team, and for two extremely good reasons. They had decided to approach Martin Hannett. Firstly, although a founding member of the Factory team, with a name as the most innovative, idiosyncratic and unpredictable record producer of the late seventies, the relationship between Hannett and Factory had fallen into a bitter and rather puerile acrimonious stalemate as the eighties progressed. The catalyst for this battle had been Factory's considerable fiscal investment in The Hacienda at the start of that decade. Hannett disliked the idea intensely from day one. He disliked discos and venues, regarding them as empty spaces in which a transient scene may or may not flourish.

71

"You don't start a scene" he reasoned "by creating empty spaces. You have to create the music first, not the venue." In the eyes of many, Hannett was absolutely correct in this assumption. It should be noted however, that his objection was not entirely without its selfish edge - for Martin Hannett, as Factory's house producer, had wanted the company to invest, not in some poxy night club, but in a Fairlight computer and studio complex. In toys basically, in toys for Martin.

Furthermore, Hannett had slipped from grace a little since his heady days at the helm of Joy Division. For instance, his final work with New Order had resulted in the artless tumble of ideas known as *Movement*, quite simply the only horrendous record the band ever made. Perhaps even more significantly, he had failed to capture the magic within both The Stone Roses and a very early version of Simply Red (who Hannett had wished to name Ghost Shirt). Maybe his legendary ear was still in place, but perhaps his indefinable genius had slipped.

Volatile and unpredictable, Hannett gave Factory a second problem. How the hell would the chemical mix, between this hedonistic innovator and the band that no-one knew how to handle, go off? Hannett made the Mondays look like choir boys on an outing - what would happen when they were thrown together? The idea thrilled and excited Nathan McGough, and it had the same effect on Ryder, who had learned all about Hannett from Barney. He too realised the friction between band and producer could be electric.

Wilson: "I loved Martin, but the thought of working with him again scared the shit out of me at first. It had been a really nasty, messy and pointless dispute, I felt, going off on a tangent over financial matters which he never really even attempted to understand. Then the more I thought about it, the more obvious it seemed. Yeah, why not? At last, we thought, we had found the right band for him. At last we had a reason to drag him out and start again. It was such a tantalising proposition and I knew that Martin wouldn't be able to resist the Mondays. Right up his street, they were. They would give him loads of drugs, wouldn't they? I knew Martin well enough to know that he wouldn't let that opportunity slip by. And it was more than that. Joy Division were a loose mess before he'd tightened the screws. You needed vision to work with Happy Mondays and if Martin had anything, he certainly had bags of vision. They would be perfect together, in one way."

Although the album was to be recorded in Hull, I distinctly remember Happy Mondays involved in a recording session with Hannett in Strawberry Studios (Tony Wilson: "That must have been a demo for the album"). I remember it because that was the night, by chance, I wandered into The Wellington pub opposite, to find Hannett, as one quite often did, crumpled at the bar. Grinning like a Cheshire cat, he was deep in conversation with some poor, befuddled and beer-soaked regular, probably talking about Stockport County or something...it didn't matter. Martin Hannett liked to play games. In particular, he liked to play games with the engineers at Strawberry who, to a man, worshipped Hannett's every absurd move. "He's a genius, he produced that track while lying on his back in the store room, reading the Beano"...etc. Hannett would often produce bands from the bar seat of The Wellington, nipping back over now and again if he felt like it, to twiddle some knob or other before swiftly darting back. That's how it was. But how would it be with the Mondays? If this was a demo session, it was costing somebody - Factory - a great deal of money. And the producer was in the pub. And The Mondays? Well, two of them had fallen into The Red Bull, further along the road, where an ex-member of Herman's Hermits was ploughing through a cabaret version of 'Cocaine'. There they were, two lads chatting to regulars, drinking pint after pint, neither of them realising for a moment that they had been deep in conversation with Merseybeat legend Wayne Fontana and ex-Manchester would-be pop star Pete McClaine from Pete McClaine And The Dakotas.

"Nice lads, they were," stated MaClaine "Happy Mondays...one of Tony Wilson's lot. Nice lads. I gave them some advice about Strawberry Studios. Trouble is, they didn't seem to care. Completely out of it, too, smashed. They have got to break with the booze or well, that's what killed Merseybeat around here. They'll either make it or they'll end up like us lot - singing in pubs, singing to each other. We have no money but we have a laugh. Happy Mondays, eh? Are they the next big thing? Someone said that the singer couldn't sing. You've gotta be able to sing, to do the business. I liked them, dressed like tramps, but at least they have a laugh. Most Strawberry bands who come in here are deadly serious."

Hannett and the band were duly dispatched to Driffield Studios in Hull, recording home of The Housemartins. It was Factory's reasoning that there was sufficient distance between Hull and The Hacienda to prevent the band members from returning to their preferred little corner each evening, peddling their E's. Alas, of course, such reasoning was to be swiftly countered by the sheer inventiveness of the band. After just two days, they discovered that an army base existed within staggering distance of their adopted local pub. Far from being phased by the nightly influx of 'squaddies', the band swiftly befriended them and, after finding they had much in common, soon began selling them E's. Before a week was up, Happy Mondays had instigated a regular and flourishing little outlet, complete with a little army-style camaraderie. Needless to say, if only for the duration of the *Bummed* recordings, that pub attained legendary status in the locality, an unlikely hot spot of laddish cheer and a strange outbreak of pre-Madchester E culture. The situation even made the local press. Although the band, mercifully perhaps, were unnamed, sadly the pub was named a "drug-den" (which probably doubled the trade that very week).

Tony Wilson: "I remember driving up to Driffield up the M62, hoping to find the band fully concentrating on the recording, which to be fair they were, but they had this little scene going. Hilarious. I couldn't believe it. Also, I couldn't believe what I encountered when I got to the studio. I remember opening the door to the recreation room, you know, the room where all the pissed musicians talk bollocks and play pool. Well, I prized this door open and it was just darkness and smoke, a kind of really thick atmosphere. And the floor was completely filled with thick, black vinyl, records just scattered everywhere, all these house records they had been playing and just casting aside. Just a thick black carpet. They had created their own little jungle. Fucking weird band, man...one fucking weird band. I remember asking Shaun what he was writing about. He just smiled and said he was writing about nothing! It shouldn't have filled me with confidence, but I'd heard 'Wrote For Luck' by then and I knew that something big was happening."

   Not quite nothing. The furiously funky and crazed single 'Wrote For Luck', destined to become the band's fourth single after the neat, swing funk of 'Twenty Four Hour Party People' was, in fact, about something very real indeed. It was nonsense, a crazy rant, stacked with neat little double meanings and innuendo. On 'Wrote For Luck', though it has often been understandably misunderstood, Shaun Ryder was singing about taking a bad trip. About bad drugs. Poison. Falling into the scary abyss as the chemicals take hold and the mind begins to darken. It was a hark back to the days when the band were truly falling through a dangerous drug nightmare. These days, having survived spells with Hannett during the recording of *Bummed*, the drug strangle-hold was beginning to loosen. "I am doing less and less now, we all are," said Shaun Ryder, "and, in fact, if we had loads of money we would probably be out water skiing, or something, hang gliding and all that crap. Drugs are just something that gets you through. I've been on a drug trip since I was twelve. Long time, mate. Knowwarrramsayin?"

   'Redneck' was another favourite from the *Bummed* sessions. Chunky country and western originally entitled 'Some Cunt From Preston'. (rhyming slang for country and western). Choppy guitars and a grumbling bass, rather quaintly described by *Melody Maker's* John Wilde as "the world's first psycho-reggae-country-western number." Only Happy Mondays, perhaps, could record such a thing. With 'Redneck', Shaun Ryder's idea was to take C&W, several miles further down the road to parody writing, in his words: "double shit corny words, a country and western song. She fell in love with me and I ran away. Haha. Romance...depends. Depends on what you call romance, mate. I call romance big boots and a big hot bed. I don't write songs for girls. You must be joking. Yeuccchhh! Cacky pooh pooh. Oh no, I've got a very ten year old attitude towards girls. The closest thing to a love song on *Bummed* is 'Being A Friend'."

Even this was not that close. Complete with lyrics pulled straight from an Amsterdam porno mag, which Shaun had one day perused whilst lying in a grubby hotel room in Amsterdam, dreaming of sex and gazing at girlies. Popping pills and drooling over acres of sweat-soaked flesh, pouting smiles, pleading, suggestive eyes. Enough to turn a man to love? It was not a love song. It was a lust song - cold and fevered, hungry and sad. And that was, in the mind of Shaun Ryder, the nearest that Happy Mondays ever came to love.

Shaun Ryder: "*Bummed*...it's fuller, man. We were more in command of what we were doin', with or without Martin. The first album was more about playing with things. Messin'. If it was up to me I wouldn't have made anything before 'Tart Tart'. I wouldn't have done that first album. That seems now like....I dunno, like something out of a daft period of childhood. Like looking at an old school essay that you now are really embarrassed by...no...no it's not that bad, but I will never be able to listen to the fuckin' thing again."

Naturally, *Bummed* was to become one of rock's great drug albums and the aforementioned claim, by the band, to have introduced E to Manchester really stems from this period. Shaun Ryder: "We was totally caned on E during the recording of *Bummed*, all of us. We'd deliberately get Martin spiked on it as well, partly because it put him in a great mood to work with and partly because it stopped him going across the road to the pub to get bladdered. We really didn't know what it was and, let's be honest, we have all learned a few hard truths about E in recent years - we were still kind of innocent about it. I was still buzzin' from me time in the Dam. I mean, we'd get up, have one about 12 o' clock, one at five, one early night time and one later on. I'm sure nobody else in Manchester was taking it before we brought it over. There was about ten of us and we'd go down the Hac and stand in the corner, all buzzin' away. It was a real crack. We were selling them for £25 a time. At first it was just a laugh, beer money and that, but it started getting serious. We weren't drug pushers. Well, maybe we were but it just happened, natural, like. They was only costing us a couple of pence each but, before long there was a massive queue of people, all dying to pay us twenty five quid a shot. It were a bit bad but I have to say we sorted all our mates out. We gave hundreds away and we was eating them like mad."

In *Arena* in 1996, Ryder expanded on this period which sits like a dark shadow in the undertone of *Bummed*: "Ecstacy changed our lives financially. It fucked us up, even as the Mondays were seeming to be going strong on the surface. We'd had a couple of years when we'd really struggled for dough. Petty pilfering, small-time drug dealing, all that lot. Me and Bez would go to them pubs where all the dancin-round-the-handbags chicks was. I'd sit at a table and me and Bez would keep talkin' and I'd have a pair of moccasins on with no socks on, right? I'd take me shoe off and open the chicks bag with me toes, get the purse out, have the money, and it'd be "see ya girls". Sometimes you'd feel a bit sorry for them and they'd have, say £60 - I tell you, man, girls always have money - so I'd take £40 and put £20 back in, so at least they would have their cab fare home."

This was the colour of their life - scrounging, sponging and thieving - to live, smoke, drink and ignore the dark brooding shadows of the true evil which has always lurked in the shadow of the Mondays (indeed, in the shadows of Salford in the eighties) - the black stain of heroin, of 'H' Where was it, with Shaun? In 1996, in the unlikely pages of *Arena*, he admitted, "I'd dabbled about the heroin since I was a 16 year old kid. I took it with me mate, first. He threw up. I didn't. But back then, I was limited by the amount of money I had. Sometimes I'd get a £5 or £10 wrap but I didn't always have the dough so that sort of naturally looked after itself. I'd have days off. But once we started getting popular with the band, me mates used to give it to me to sample, so there was plenty about. I've hit up, I've had a dig, yeah, but I don't like, *do* it...it's the worst drug in the world and shouldn't be touched. The dirtiest, nastiest, most evil shite ever. Really fucking horrible."

Fax to Factory office from French rock promoter. March 1988. "I've got many problems with the band. First, they destroy hotel in Grenoble. Second, they don't want to play on night of 20th in Paris. I never received cancellation for this. Third, they get in trouble in a club, La Palace in Paris. Fourth, very big fighting during concert at Rennes between band, local promoter and my tour manager."

The face...the face

It was at a run of the mill Factory meeting at their Victorian headquarters, that the Factory team - Tony Wilson, Alan Erasmus, Rob Gretton and Tina Simmons - fell into a discussion about a possible fly poster campaign for *Bummed*. Ever since Pete Saville's stark, evocative graphics had graced Factory poster art in the late seventies, transforming the dull, crude, often vacuous rock poster into a work of art, the company had suffered from a few predictable problems. It may seem obvious, in retrospect, to point this out, but Factory posters had always typified the company's approach to promotion and, as such, had highlighted their shortcomings. What is bound to happen, for example, if you create a rock poster of genuine aesthetic worth and you pepper the walls of any major British city with it? Easy. The posters will become instantly collectable and, in the words of one Factory director "the little bastards will tear the things down and put them up in their fucking bedrooms." Certain Factory posters, attempting to convey the date and location of New Order gigs were peeled from the walls in their entirety before the glue had been allowed to dry. The posters for *Bummed* - the stunning Central Station-designed colour-flushed face, would almost certainly suffer a similar fate. Their seemed little point in peppering Manchester in the traditional way. Something outrageous needed to be done.

It was around this time that Factory had, unwisely as it would turn out, started to dabble in property development by purchasing a ramshackle slug of a building on Charles Street, directly behind the BBC. The intention was to use the skills of Hacienda designer Ben Kelly to transform this unlikely building into a pristine new Factory office. Alan Erasmus, as sharp as ever, realised that the huge volume of commuter traffic heading out of the city centre towards the south Manchester arteries would, at one point, be driving directly towards this previously ignored and lonely building. To an opportunist's mind, this made it far more valuable than a soot-blackened mess of bricks and mortar. It was a giant hoarding, simply begging to be adorned with posters. Erasmus reasoned that if the building could be smothered from top to toe with the *Bummed* 'faces', then the end result would be both stunningly surreal and frankly unmissable. In this simple, effective way, Factory created a new instant, cheap Manchester landmark. The faces which leered so mockingly at the bank clerks, building society workers and hi-fi sales people who filtered slowly past it twice daily, would collectively form a defiant rave symbol. The first outing, perhaps, of the culture that would become known as 'Madchester'. Probably the first identifiable symbol of a Manchester dance culture.

There were other promotional idiosyncrasies with *Bummed*. The title, for instance, proved to be somewhat less offensive than was initially intended. Shaun Ryder: "It was just a stupid, silly little sick stupid name. We wanted it to be offensive and we thought loads of people would take it the wrong way." They did, indeed, take it the wrong way by largely failing to notice anything offensive about it at all. 'Bummed' can, in various connotations, mean anything from the obvious cadging (i.e. he bummed a fag from his mate) to scrounging a room for the night (he bummed a carpet) or, of course, the cruder context. Perhaps to accentuate their intent to irritate, Central Station Design placed a picture of a naked woman on the inner sleeve. Not perhaps, in these post-*Loaded* days where anything goes, a particularly striking example of laddish aggression, but this was Manchester in 1988. The city was still held captive under the tyranny of the shorn-haired, green shoe-d 'rad fems' of Chorlton Cum Hardy - into the Town Hall they surged, taking up battle positions on more committees than you would imagine could possibly exist. In the eyes of this self-righteous and somewhat poisonous rainbow-jumpered bunch, sticking a naked woman on your inner sleeve is tantamount to starting a full scale sex war. Hilarious, ludicrous, pathetic, but that's how it was. Pop hack Penny Anderson, writing for *City Life* magazine opined "I'm annoyed, not outraged, just irritated. Not at the sight of nudity, no, not at that but I don't need to gratuitously observe anyone else's. Look here little boys, and I mean all of you, if you want to build up your wrist muscles, do it in the privacy of your own home, not your design offices." The *NME*'s Mandi James was no more forgiving: "There's no point being dewy eyed. Shaun Ryder can't sing. They are a sloppy unit, and their attitude towards women sucks. They're sexist wankers. The thing I resent most about the whole Manchester scene is that it's very male. Not like punk, where women came to the front, with Slits, Siouxsie..."

Despite this rather neurotic controversy, despite the very mixed press notices, despite the subsequently huge music press features and, most of all, despite the buzz in the city of Manchester, initial sales of *Bummed* were hugely disappointing. Factory, however, were not immediately concerned. After all, this was 1988 and, twelve months previously the label had been shunted on to a new and somewhat unexpected plateau. A New Order double compilation album, *Substance*, initially constructed as nothing more than a handy compilation tape for Tony Wilson to listen to on his long car drives, had somehow evolved into New

Order's biggest selling album, shifting 400,000 copies in Britain alone that year. The record instigated the mighty hit single 'True Faith', thereby shuffling Factory, and for that matter, New Order, merrily up the grand scheme of things. However, the success of *Substance* also worried Tony Wilson. At a Factory meeting, instead of basking in the glory, he spelt out the warning signs: "*Substance* has provided us with one big fucking problem," he wisely stated, "in that it has made us safe, at least for the time being. But we are in grave danger, right now, of just sitting here and becoming fat dinosaurs, totally up our own arses, not seeing what's going on. We are doing well, but something else is going to happen. It always does. We must keep our ears and eyes open."

Wilson fully acknowledged that, in truth, he wasn't particularly adept at spotting the surge of energy at source, but he had always been lucky enough to be able to capitalise on it fairly swiftly - Joy Division, New Order, OMD had practically fallen into his lap. He did know that, when it happened, when the full surge began, it would always seem to be kicked into action just when it was least expected. That day he glanced at the sales figures of all his Factory acts - a mixed bag, topped, of course, by New Order. Despite his faith in the Mondays, he would have been astonished to discover that the next violent surge of youth culture - if one can forgive that horrible phrase - had already begun. Deep within the swirl of street mythology that surrounded his own Swinton scruffs.

It had already started. Back there, as 1988 slowed to a halt. In the Hacienda, you could sense it. You could see it, on stage, with Bez, above all, with Bez. A man who one day would be so stupidly described by Tom Hibbert, who really should have known better, as "a great clod." But Bez wasn't a clod. He was there, right in there, Bez was the heart, the catalyst; it began with him, on stage at The Hacienda, standing in a daze, dancing without moving his legs, his two arms wavering upwards, like upturned octopus tentacles, reaching for something. Then there was that face, glazed, tranced, as if the soul had left and was hovering somewhere above. The strange new age of something spiritual. Bez, not a dancer, but a leader. No words, no tunes, no music, just a body rhythm, jerking, away, encouraging a new age and a new stance. Initially just a pose, but then more, much more. So ironically intelligent. People watched, entranced. Yes, in Bez, there really was some kind of enigma. He was simply born to be wavering away alongside Shaun, counter-acting that gruffness, adding an extra dimension. Bez was the man who lifted the dance floors, added some kind of spice, took the Hacienda onto a new level that was so far away from its black 'n' white rockist beginnings. The so-called 'Second Summer of Love' in 1987 that had married the sixties with the eighties, had been a mere precursor. This was a new dance, alright and so much more besides.

Factory, in general, had absolutely no idea what was going on. There they were, pushing away with the Mondays, half-wondering whether or not they really were flogging a dead horse. After all, at face value, Happy Mondays were poor funk clap trap, some kind of chunder. One of the people watching and listening, and becoming increasingly inspired, was New Order's Barney Sumner, always a man who could spot something worthwhile in embryonic form. It was Happy Mondays who drew Barney out of the alcoves, stripped him of his essential pop star aura of cool, dragged him on to the dance floor where he moved and moved, arms raised high, a rooted octopus. Like Bez.

And it was Barney Sumner who paid the ultimate compliment, on *Top Of The Pops*. This was a full year before the mighty occasion when Happy Mondays and The Stone Roses would appear on the same show, effectively cementing the cult of Madchester. Here, twelve months before, were New Order, punching away through 'Prime Time', with Barney dancing away in a full-blooded Bez parody. The new age had begun, and Barney had shown the way. Factory, dimmed by business and living the life, hadn't even noticed it. Wilson was wrong. The new wave wasn't something which they should have been looking out for. It was something they had already captured.

CHAPTER 8

"We're obsessed with sex. It's to do with dirty women down Little Hulton, 35 year old divorcees with two kids, who give you warts. I've still got a very big one to prove it."

Shaun Ryder

Cats 'n' rats

John Wilde was at the same time both the best and the worst person to get an interview out of the violent, unpretentious, grinning, gawping, swearing beast that was Happy Mondays. Generally considered a 'good egg', Wilde had trawled the punk streets of Camden in mock leopard skins and leather like a latter-day no-future Puck. Moving from the ill-fated *Jamming* magazine to the more intellectual heights of *Sounds*, he came ultimately to *Melody Maker*, brimming with ideas and notions of what made for great music, great writing and how the two could be brought together.

He dragged perhaps the best piece ever written about the Mondays out of an interview in a London hotel. He was the rock journalist escaped from a mundane up-bringing Wales. They were the next big thing, still scampering after any exposure they could get. Wilde had noted how dull The Stone Roses were. No chance of repeating that observation with regards to this wayward bunch of Mancunians.

Shaun Ryder sat, as he often would, looking like a tramp sheltering from the cold in the plush surrounds of a London hotel. He was talking. People, shuffling nervously, were casting dubious glances. The kind of glances that people would eternally cast towards Happy Mondays. His gruff tones slicing through the atmosphere. Barely worth listening to, in that coffee lounge, but well worth recording here.

Glimpse here, then, into a vision of a Little Hulton childhood: "We used to go ratting. Our house was behind a sewage farm.

We used to shoot 'em with air pistols. Great fun (a woman in a red cashmere sweater shuffles nervously, Shaun sniffs twice...continues). Ever looked behind a sewage farm? It stinks. You gotta have somewhere to play. You do those things when you are 12 or 13. You see all these rats running about. So the only thing to do is start shooting them. Rats. It's okay to kill 'em."

Wilde, at this point, disgraced himself by comparing rats to cats. Ryder: "Cats are different. Kids who go around spearing cats are just dickheads. Cats are top. Cats talk and everything. They can talk to you. I've just read a book. In the book, right, it tells you what they mean. Like they go 'Meeeiowww' and that means, 'let me out, I've 'ad me food." Look mate...I'm not gonna knock ya. I might come round to your house and you'll have all these rats running around. You'll show me how to talk to them. I'm not going to call you a dickhead. If you can prove to me that those rats are alright, I'll get into it. But I don't like rats, I don't mind sayin'. There's a difference, see, between wild white rats and 'orrible, squirmy, scumbag gyppo rats that run around in fields and live in sewage farms. You don't have to feel sorry for rats. They can eat your brains out. You don't have to feel sorry for summat that can do that to ya."

That little exchange remains hugely typical of Happy Mondays' approach. It is, of course, bereft of pretension and was delivered with heartfelt sincerity, with Ryder talking like an overly serious schoolboy pushed into a strange train of thought, seemingly unaware that his witterings would enlighten that week's issue of *Melody Maker*.

It proved, to the gleefully befuddled Wilde that perhaps not everyone is a pseud. That conversation could just as easily have taken place between Ryder and some sales rep he might meet on the old Inter City. There is no front. No angle, other than a natural, impish bent towards setting a new scam in motion. The Happy Mondays experience - a singularly cock-eyed affair. I interviewed two of them at the time of *Bummed*, and found myself pinballing around a thousand topics, none of which had ever seemed remotely interesting before but, in the company of the Mondays, gained a curious relevance: "We are not weird" Shaun stated, "some people say that we are weird because we're different from other bands. Because we talk a load of shite, sometimes, but those people don't know us, do they? We are not really weird, are we? We've never been weird. We're not in a daze. You can't be in a daze all the time, can ya? You gotta know what you are doing. We all know...and reality? What the fuck is that, man? I don't even think about that. As far as I'm concerned, I'm not interested. I'm not interested in dying people. I don't give a fuck about anybody else. I'm interested in me, my mates. I couldn't give a dong about anyone else. As far as I'm concerned, I want them to build loads of top space ships so we can start looking at proper planets and stop fucking about doing stupid things here."

Then he stopped to reconsider: "Actually, that's a dumb, horrible thing to say. If someone dying came up to me, I'd help them. But you really have to look after yourself and your mates. If a load of Ethiopians were dying in the park over there, I'd do my best to help them. I'd have a go at it, 'cos, I don't like to see anybody like that. Especially families. But I'm not gonna get into all that bollocks 'cos I've not got time for it and it's just not my world."

"I wouldn't say we were ahead of our time. I wouldn't go out and say that. I can say there's no one quite like us, when I know whose music we rip off. We rip off everybody. No exceptions. I can't tell you who, though. Paul Daniels doesn't give his secrets away, does he? Basically, we don't know what the rules are supposed to be. I can't say we consciously go out to copy summat. We end up doing fings what are stored in our heads. We put it out our own way, like. If I was to copy a picture, any picture, then what I would do would look fuck all like the original. But I'd still be stealing in a way. That's what we do with songs. See, a lot of bands copy in a really obvious way. That's really fucking stupid because they just end up like some shite parody, or whatever. To be really honest, we couldn't do it anyway. We tried, we were a copy band once and our cover versions were shite. I sounded like the world's worst pub singer. So you have to use a bit of nouse and get by. If that's foolin' people...so what? Maybe it is."

Maybe it is, but, as Ryder eloquently stated, so what? All the best rock 'n' roll acts have been clever copyists, from Reed to Zep, from the Stones to the Pistols. But, even if the intention is to steal and warp, which is exactly what the Mondays were fantastic at, it has to be done with some style, with some degree of professionalism. Yes? Shaun? Ryder: "We admire professionalism, man. Our attitude is just that we don't do anything for anybody if we don't wanna. If we are in a bad mood, we don't do the concert. That might be unprofessional but it can't be done, can it? None of us grew up with discipline. We can't get into it. Like these lads who come from the army on leave. They're going "It's fucking great, man. The sarge made me stand on one leg in the corner for three hours with me hand behind me 'ead and balancing a cherry on me nose." I mean, well, what a dickhead. If they like discipline, that's them. But there is no way any cunt would have me stood on one leg with a cherry on me nose, just 'cos the sarge said so."

CHAPTER 9

Madchester...faint stirrings

In January, 1989, the scene that became known to the world as 'Madchester' had started to speed up. It had been evolving, one might say, since the mid-eighties when, amongst others, New Order suddenly found themselves playing to British crowds of a surprisingly disparate and far more volatile nature than usual. Gone, it seemed, were the legions of heavily over-coated 'indie-heads', and, even in university towns, their hardcore student following had been greatly diluted by an influx of Nike clad teens, who adopted previously mentioned dull tags like Perry Boys (and girls). It was a mod-ish swing towards the working class that would eventually result in 'scallydelia' (another daft, dull tag). In Manchester, if not elsewhere, the music scene was being reclaimed. Following New Order's links with the dance scene of New York (which began with 1993's Arthur Baker produced 'Confusion') and booker/DJ Mike Pickering's frequent sortés to the house scene of Chicago, The Hacienda had become the home of a hugely innovative swell of DJ-ing featuring people like Graeme Parke and Dave Haslam. The dance floors steadily filled until, during the peak in the heady days of 1990, it would become the world's premier dance club.

The full extent of this remarkable transition, which effectively abolished the barriers between indie and dance (and, indeed, between rock and disco, a vacuous war which had raged since the mid-seventies) wasn't really apparent at the start of 1989, when those who would surf the Madchester explosion were still immersed in a messy and furiously competitive local scene. This messiness was perhaps most apparent with the situation that lurked darkly behind the stuttering rise of Inspiral Carpets. Initially a psychedelic garage outfit from Oldham, Inspirals had been battling furiously for some kind of national breakthrough since 1986. Via a couple of distinctively powerful EP's on Paula Greenwood's Playtime Records, they had evolved into natural stalwarts of Radio One's *John Peel Show*. Following the departure of their singer, however, the Inspirals - always more industrious that industrial - had wrenched themselves away from Playtime, leaving Greenwood debt-ridden and bitter. By the start of 1989, after fending off vicious rumours from all quarters, they embarked on a rapid rise to the dizzy heights in the slipstream of the Mondays and The Stone Roses.

In January 1989, as the Inspirals were merely licking their wounds and regrouping, The Stone Roses were being whisked around the houses of local journalists in the back of their manager, Gareth Evans' Range Rover. Meanwhile, Happy Mondays were headlining at Panic Station's birthday celebration bash at The Kilburn National Ballroom, a prestigious 'top spot' in the capital. Soon afterwards, Shaun and Bez were busted. Ryder was detained in Jersey after traces of cocaine had been found in his pockets whilst Bez was fined an outrageous £700 for the possession of cannabis. Both busts would be reported in the music press but neither would hint at the kind of tabloid frenzy that would affect the band in later days.

Fucking Advocaat!

The Factory-based film-makers The Bailey Brothers conceived a notion whereby the Mondays would be put together with sixties star Karl Denver. The idea was to come up with a short film that would precede their epic feature *Mad Fuckers*, a subversive tale of a Salford gang who stole a Jaguar and in a confusion of speed-fuelled madness, ended up driving it through a ballroom wall in Blackpool. The feature, later re-titled *Bad Move*, saw Tony Wilson at one point virtually begging the moguls of Hollywood to invest in the venture. The Bailey Brothers wanted to make a short film about the similar real-life adventures of the Mondays, including the lovely idiosyncratic Denver for added flavour. The film was to be called *One Armed Boxer*. Out of this was also planned a re-make of the melodic and autobiographical pop song 'Lazyitis'.

Denver was committed to a cabaret contract in Jersey, so on Monday, McGough and Ryder flew out to meet him. Ryder was due back by Wednesday for a television appearance, but planned to catch Denver's show, meet him afterwards, charm the pants off him and having bagged the liaison, get back to the mainland as soon as possible.

At 11 am, Tuesday morning, the panicked, disembodied tones of Nathan McGough could be heard ranting away in the ear-piece of Tony Wilson's telephone" "Shaun's been arrested," he screamed (an alarming although not altogether unfamiliar sentence), followed by an indecipherable barrage, heavily punctuated by obscenities i.e. Fucking twat, fucking caught, traces coke in fucking pocket, maan, daft fucker, police chief, slammed in jail, what the fuck do we do..." Wilson replaced the receiver and waited for the next call which came at 11.30 am. "It's okay, it's sorted," explained a rather calmer McGough. "We've got a local lawyer on the case, all will be okay, we'll get Shaun off the island. No problem. Sorted." The only problem was that it wasn't sorted at all. Ryder, who, following his admittedly irritating bust, had imploded somewhat, now only seemed capable of uttering two words repeatedly: "Fuck off, fuck off, fuck off" when asked if he would like to see a lawyer. Even McGough seemed baffled by this latest little twist. Once the pair had managed to wrench themselves from the tight grip of the island's would-be Bergeracs, and only after they had settled on a plane that was clearly over the sea, did he pose the question that had been bugging him all morning: "Shaun" he tentatively enquired, "I hope you don't mind me asking, but, why did you refuse to see a lawyer, back there?" The reply came back: "Fucking lawyers...didn't want to see no fucking lawyer...didn't want to see no fuckin' nobody, don't be stupid...fuckin' lawyers...fuckin' cunts!" Realising that Ryder hadn't, in truth, allowed any space for further investigation,

McGough shrugged and sat back. Shortly after, he was awakened by Ryder who, it seemed, now wished to talk: "They were fucking weird man," he stated, apropos of nothing. "Who, Shaun?" enquired McGough. "Those cunts, man," said Ryder, "those Jersey cops, they were really fucking weird man, couldn't work them out at all. Y'know what, they kept offering me drinks, man. Fucking kept opening the door, offering me drinks. Fucking weird that is, man, fucking weird cops or what? They kept sayin' to me, "Mr Ryder, do you want an Advocaat?" I said, "Fuuuuck offf!". Fucking hate fuckin' Advocaat, maan."

1989, Fun and Wheels

Tony Wilson: "There is nothing worse than the Mondays on tour. They are impossible. Brilliant and impossible. I love them and I want to kill them. When you expect them to be good, they are shit. When they need to work hard, they are as lazy as fuck and, just when you are about to give up on them, they produce a stormer. Just like New Order. Funny, that."

Derek Ryder: "We always took a Manc attitude with us. What's that phrase? Hook 'em an' fuck 'em? That was us. Get on and get out as quickly as possible. Forty minutes max. Get back in the bar. We always had problems in America with that attitude. Made you sick, the Yanks, always wanting some kind of rock show. I mean, what did they think it was?"

In March, 1989, Happy Mondays set forth from their lowly cellar at The Boardwalk, to sample the considerable and under-rated delights of Belfast. Always a great gig, especially in the old days when audiences would fall together in mass slam-dance. To the uninitiated, this was seemingly a scary ocean of folk, teetering on the peak of mob violence. What would they make of the Mondays?

In the event, Belfast never got the full picture anyway. As the band mingled with the business suits and holiday-makers in Manchester's airport's departure lounge, the police descended upon the hapless, dazed crew and snapped up Bez on what he later referred to as "some fuckin' bail fuckin' mix up...fucking hassles, maan."

Hassles indeed, but hassles that perhaps showed the Mondays, and Bez's contribution to them, in their true light. Without him they were naked, rag-taggle and dim. His charisma, his enigma, was that of a star, and without this star the Mondays failed to shine in Belfast. Whatever 'it' was that Bez had, it was painfully obvious that the band needed it if they were going to stand head and shoulders above the rest of the scene.

In 1996, I came across Bez and TV pundit Terry Christian in Manchester's Atlas bar. Christian was the name of the moment, one of a new generation of presenters that the media loved to hate, but in this climate, man against man, it was clearly Bez who sparkled, who drew the admiring glances from passers-by. "There's Bez", they whispered, with no mention of Christian.

The Mondays recognised what he meant to them as a band on that March night in Belfast, 1989. The gig lasted just twenty minutes, their finale 'Twenty Four Hour Party People' leaving the audience open-mouthed, barely warmed up.

Melody Maker's Ian Gittins was on hand. As they trundled offstage, and as a growl began to emanate from the audience, he posed a simple question. "Are you a bunch of weirdo's?" Answer (It could have been Shaun...or Paul): "No. We are not wearing a check suit. We haven't got an MG or a gravel path."

Two days later, the band found themselves amid the celebratory chaos of Dublin on St. Patrick's Day. The perfect situation, perhaps. A hedonistic city swallowing a hedonistic band. After tripping, literally it seemed, across the border, and not arriving until 2am, the Mondays chose to keep the curtains shut tight. Shaun Ryder, in particular, did not wish to rise from his pit until at the earliest twenty minutes before the gig at McGonagles Club.

"Are you similar people?" That was a good question. Wish I'd asked it, but it belonged, again, to Ian Gittins. Impossible to answer, for in many ways the Happy Mondays were not only similar, they were one. And then again, look at them. Shaun of course. Gary Whelan, speed-mouth, loud and proud. Paul Ryder (Horse), quieter, happily reserved, standing in the Ryder family shadows. And Mark Day (Cow), aloof, funny in a way that is always a little strange. And Paul, healthily surreal.

Ian Gittins had asked the question - this is the bizarre reply he received:

"Some of us are short. Some of us are tall."

"It could have been the six form, or lower."

Gaz: "Yeah, dead normal, us."

Paul: "You're thick."

Gaz: "Thick?"

Paul: "Very thick. How many times, last night, did you leave the door open? Every door you went through?"

Gaz: "What's that got to do with being thick?"

Paul: "When it's like, your own door."

Hardly, one might suggest, one of the great conversations of our time - it is perhaps understandable that the band always seemed happy to allow Shaun (although no great orator himself), to handle the verbals. Interestingly enough, almost every Happy Mondays interview ever conducted has tended to follow the very same course. A great hefty stream of nonsensical guff from Shaun Ryder, liberally peppered with absurd interjections from each member of the band, pushing and pulling Shaun this way and that. Rather like their live set.

The Dublin gig proved infinitely superior to the Belfast debacle. Not that that was too difficult, but at least this time they tried. Ryder, in particular, compensated for the great hole where Bez should have been, by pounding the stage in mock despotic antics: "Play some bass, you cunt" he scolded Paul, who merely grinned in defiance "Go on...play some fucking bass...pleeeease the crowd!" It was like Mark E Smith minus the charm. Like Barney Sumner minus the audience rapport.

One week later, with their Bez-less Irish excursions just a memory, Happy Mondays dutifully turn out at Birmingham's vast, cavernous N.E.C. to partake in their time-honoured role as support act to New Order. A similar gig, at Manchester's G-Mex back in December, had seen the band looking woefully lost amongst the shadows and the muddy sound. This time, the situation looked even worse. The band crashed into their set with spirited aplomb and sounded like a series of butterfly farts in an oil drum. Somewhere, over at the end, a little band was playing...and it did seem little, too. Until, that is, the sound crew remembered to turn the sound up and the funk stretched its limbs and began affecting people. And, just as a few ripples of excitement began to stir the giant (10,000 plus) crowd, it was, of course, all over. Most of the crowd remained bemused, thinking only of New Order. Happy Mondays had come and had gone, simply supplying a swift imprint on the audiences memory. Most of their gigs were like that. Short, sharp shocks.

Were they being extremely clever here, or extremely lazy, or both? From here, few would have predicted that within a year, the Happy Mondays party would take control of these stadiums in its own right. Certainly not Shaun Ryder. Backstage, that night he sat, his despondent head held in his arms, while Nathan McGough attempted to console him.: "It wasn't crap, man, it was just the sound, it did you no favours." "Oh, thanks a fucking lot, man, cunt, man." replied Ryder. Over in the corner, Bez was lying on the floor, staring at the ceiling, dreaming of being somewhere else. In the distance came the distant rumble of Pete Hook's guiding bass.

Madchester

It was, at first, a marketing joke. In time it would twist into a horrendous nightmare, but for now the word and concept of 'Madchester' was fantastically relevant to the time. And it wasn't invented by the music press. The *NME*'s Danny Kelly, among others, would claim the honour of instigating 'Madchester'. Factory would hotly dispute this. Keith Jobing stated: "It was fucking always a Factory thing. In fact, for better or worse, we copyrighted the word 'Madchester'. That was it. I don't know what Kelly had to do with it at all." In the beginning there were three daft T-shirts. One read, "Just say no to London", a curiously vicious little angle on the government run anti-heroin campaign. Then came "Madchester. Nigell Madsell, From The Isle Of Mad." Which was, to say the least, odd. And finally, the self explanatory, "Mad Fuckers". Initially, this was put to the Mondays as a loose concept that might, or might not, surround the campaign for their forthcoming 'A Madchester EP'.

In the Factory office, the band laughed and then, sensing that the sheer daftness might work, finally agreed. Predictably, however, as Tony Wilson met up with them three days later, in the Factory-owned Dry Bar, the band's decision had been completely reversed: "Madchester, that's a stupid concept, a stupid thing, we don't like it, we don't want anything to do with that. Madchester..leave it with us, Tony, we'll think up something far better than that. Stupid idea, Madchester, hah!" "Hey lads, it's too late," lied Wilson, "the T-shirts have already gone to the printers. It would cost the Earth to reverse them. Madchester man, it's great. Get to like it because you are stuck with it now. Sorry lads but you are the first Madchester band."

And so Madchester would appear, initially on a series of promotional post cards, featuring sober visions of Manchester sights - Madchester Piccadilly Station, Madchester University, Madchester United F.C, a deliberately bland rave vision creeping into the city's consciousness. Long before the band had cemented their ground-breaking 'Madchester E.P', it had become a regular word in the ironically Madchester-crazed music press. It was a simple word but, somehow, it captured the feel. The Madchester rave scene was up and running. For better or for worse. the city would never be quite the same again.

Happy Mondays, without quite knowing how they had managed it, were perched at the peak of this new, hastily assembled hierarchy.

CHAPTER 10

America, Summer 1989, Los Angeles

L.A. suited the Mondays, if not vice versa. The jacuzzi at the hotel, for a start, was situated within staggering distance of their rooms. Most rock bands, upon entering L.A. for the first time, are instantly introduced to the kind of Mexican dope that makes you melt from the head down, draining your strength away, transforming your limbs to rubber, nullifying your thoughts, heightening your paranoia. Happy Mondays grasped this stuff with ferocious enthusiasm. It soon became a favourite pastime, taking three 'pulls' each and losing the sensation of having, or needing legs, or arms, or brains. The entire band would be just sitting poolside, apparently dead to the world, jabbering away in nonsensical tones. Paranoia running high, cabbages trapped inside their heads, unable to communicate in any kind of noticeable human manner.They had intended, that night, to go up Sunset Boulevard, to catch the movie *Batman*, but, when push came to shove, not one member of the band could manage even the slightest movement. Mondays, frozen to stone, in L.A.

Paul Ryder: "We've caned some bush in our time but never like this Mexican gear we got. It was instant death. That's why you see films of Mexicans always slumped with their heads on their chests. It's the weed that does it. Kills you stone dead. You couldn't exist for long on that stuff. Imagine smoking it for thirty years."

America, we have so often been told, never 'got' the Mondays. Quite frankly, one could understand that. After all, when you have produced James Brown and George Clinton, why would you allow time to listen to a bunch of Mancunian scruffs and their ramshackle funk? For a while however, America did, indeed, 'get' the Mondays. The day after their first connection with that Mexican gear, Happy Mondays played to a sell-out crowd of dancing, prancing lunatics and luminaries, all mixing together, all fighting to join the party. Maybe it just seemed like the hip thing to do, but they were all there, the infamous Sunset Strip liggers, all crazed in the normal Californian manner, this time including the likes of David Bowie, The Beastie Boys and various members of Guns 'n' Roses. Each endured a typical tongue lashing from drummer Gaz, who spent much of the evening running around David Bowie, exclaiming to the exasperated gathering of post-gig sycophants, "Look at the fuckin' state of him (Bowie). He's a right fuckin' midget, he is. What a complete dwarf! What a cunt!" It could, of course, have been the weed talking. "Nah," Shaun would later explain, "It was just Gaz. He's a right fucking cunt. Always slagging people off. So it was Bowie, oh, and he had a go at Axl Rose did he. Oh well, he probably deserved it."

Paul on Nathan: "It's not surprising that we get into a few scrapes when our manager is a bigger fuckin' idiot than you are. He's just as bad as us, that cunt. He's supposed to be in LA on business, but really he's just spending thirty grand on the American Express card. Pure partying. He's a proper blagger, that cunt."

It had been a good tour. All the band agreed. Not 'good' in the sense that all the gigs were successes. Indeed, very few of the gigs managed to survive in any of the band's collective memories, but it was good in the sense that it had been a blag. Even the strongest Mexican dope, for instance, couldn't fog out the fun the band had, while "tryin' ta 'unt down some E in this stupid country." Their little adventures climaxed in Cleveland, Ohio. While cruising in their hired car, tripping around the areas that had been singled out for their drug possibilities, a black gang had leapt on to their vehicle and proceeded to batter it to bits with their extensive collection of baseball bats. This had followed an incident which saw Ryder becoming involved with a couple of members of the legendary Grateful Dead 'family', who had supplied him with some "wild stuff". This unlikely little liaison had resulted in Ryder standing alone, dead centre of a highway, flagging down a fearsome juggernaut, screaming, "I'm English and I'm tripping, so please take me home." The two congenial black guys helped him into the cab and took him to Cleveland. The incident was reported in the *New York Times* although, with a tabloid-esque disregard for the truth, the whole affair had been strangely 'shifted' to Harlem. "Nah, Harlem was a different scare," explained Paul Ryder "I think we were just 'anging about with some black geezers and one of them turned nasty on us. Sommat like that. But it were no different than Salford." Another report told the story of how Shaun, wallowing in a bad trip, missed a gig because of having to have his stomach pumped. This was hotly denied by the band who quaintly explained, "He just had to go and get some more shots for the clap...just in case."

*   *   *

"So how was America, chaps?" asked Tony Wilson. He had parked his Jaguar on Oldham Street, where it seemed violently conspicuous, and had sauntered into Dry Bar as if he owned the place. Which, of course, he did...in part. Unlike the members of New Order, who also had shares in Dry Bar and tended to melt perfectly into place next to the average punters, Wilson, with his sharp Japanese suits, his unmistakable, dominating voice, his celebrated eloquence, his TV fame and his record business infamy, always looked a league apart. Nobody could mistake him. He was Tony Wilson.

Happy Mondays were giggling, as per usual, as Wilson approached them. Like cheeky schoolboys watching their headmaster saunter down the corridor, they dubbed him "Fat Willy" and chortled drunkenly, gazing down upon their array of lager bottles, their overflowing ash trays, their collapsing tables and upturned chairs. Dry Bar manager Leroy Richardson, who had dutifully worked his way up the Factory ladder, from a lowly position of Hacienda drinks collector to a valued member of the Factory team, had just about reached the end of his tether with the Mondays. Time was when a band, a famous local Factory band, would be heartily encouraged to spend time in the bar, acting as they did, as a magnet for gawping fans. That may have worked with New Order, with The Stone Roses and, in time, it would work with Oasis. But Happy Mondays had become a serious problem. Their looseness, their apparent lack of concern for property was infectious. Not for the first or last time, Leroy Richardson had threatened to ban Happy Mondays. Wilson would duly apologise for the band and leave for a meeting with record distributors in Brighton. Shaun Ryder would grin like a Cheshire cat, and utter something along the lines of the Pythonesque "stupid git". Within an hour he would turn to 808 State member Graham Massey - once the guiding light behind Factory act Biting Tongues, latterly a leading figure in the world of Madchester - and throw up all over Massey's trousers before spiralling to the ground in a drunken stupor.

"Jeeez, Shaun, for fucking Christ's sake," screamed Richardson and Massey, no doubt-organising for a mop to be duly ushered into use. Bez, proudly sporting a wound on his left hand as a result of falling through his window whilst trying to break into his own flat after losing his keys, chose that moment to burst into a fit of dope-fuelled giggles. Everything seemed normal. That night Shaun Ryder would piss on somebody's drawers.

The next day, as witnessed by the *NME*'s Jack Barron, was a normal Monday's Monday, with Shaun Ryder staggering into the dank office of Playhard Records, deep in a dusty Victorian office complex. He grasped two beer bottles and, after ripping the caps away with his teeth, handed one to Barron. A normal day. Indeed, a happy day. Preparations were being made for the band to jet off on various holidays, holidays away from each other. Shaun to Ibiza, Paul to Rimini, Bez to Amsterdam (naturally). Meanwhile, Shaun explained a little more about the American tour where, apparently, they carved out a cult following among acid-crazed Vietnam vets.

"PCP! It's alright but it's dangerous gear. We had a good time on it but I can imagine fucking flippin' out on it. It sent me a bit off me shed. I was trying to lift cars up, lift up anything, in fact. I remember walking down the road and trying to snatch gold off the black kids. I should have been shot."

The legacy of the previous evening would soon close in on Shaun. He received a phone call, and then another, and then another. Disembodied voices were screaming in his ear. Girls, boys...mates! Ryder had wandered around Dry Bar explaining, in deep, earnest tones to his mates, just how their girlfriends had been misbehaving with other guys. Ruptions, ruptions.

Ryder: "Oh so what! If I can't do a cunty deed once in a while then I'm finished. You've got to do something really cunty once a week to keep you on your toes."

"Cunty" perhaps, might be a good word to describe Shaun's demeanour the day that Tony Wilson, forever pushing Granada into installing music and youth elements into their regular programming, managed to set up a feature for a children's TV programme in which Happy Mondays would chat about the strange business of being in a pop band. It was no big deal. A minor item in a literally minor programme, complete with a live audience of giggly little kids, all high on the strange glamour of a TV studio, which was full of 'kiddy' ambience. The questions, naturally, were suitably banal: "How did you become a group? What's it like to play on telly?" Ryder settled into the serious business of enjoying himself, on camera, in front of the kids...and live. Shaun was then asked how important it was for the band to have a manager.

"Well, it's alright, man," he replied, before, thinking a bit and adding "except that ours is such a fucking Jew."

CHAPTER 11

The Nasty Nineties

One of the most successful hard dance singles of all-time snuck out in 1989. 'Ride On Time' by Black Box, with the assistance of former Factory and Hacienda man Mike Pickering, kept the No.1 slot in Britain for six weeks. It was controversial, irresistible, but most poignantly, it signalled that the world was ready for dance music again, that rave culture was mainstream, and that anything was possible. Tony Wilson, among others, felt that the great music decade of the nineties began during those six weeks.

In the eleventh hour of 1989, something else transpired that would serve to shape the face of the nineties. The two great Manchester bands of the era, Happy Mondays and The Stone Roses, melted together in a one night orgy of camaraderie, and much else besides, invading the *Top Of The Pops* studio with simultaneous hit singles. On hand, to witness this momentous event, was notorious *Face* writer, Nick Kent. His subsequent article however, made much of an off-hand remark that Tony Wilson insists he never made, and soured relations between *The Face* and Factory, between *The Face* and Madchester and between Kent and just about everyone involved. The article insisted that Wilson stated, "I have no problem whatsoever with any of these guys dying on me. Listen, Ian Curtis dying on me was the greatest thing that ever happened in my life. Death sells." Wilson, fending off a barrage of protest from, among others, Ian Curtis' wife Deborah, resolutely denied the quote and demanded that *The Face* send him a copy of the tape. No tape ever arrived and so from this it could be deduced that Wilson never made the statement. On the other hand, and in fairness to Nick Kent, even if a tape did exist then he would surely be instructed, by *The Face*'s lawyers, not to send a copy to Wilson, for that would surely be playing straight into enemy hands. As the Paris based Kent still insists that a tape exists, we will probably never know the truth. The article should have been a *celebration*, rather than this sordid mess which eventually saw *Face* editor Sheryl Garrett apologising to Tony Wilson and admitting that Kent was entirely the wrong person to handle such a situation.

Kent, famous for fifteen minutes for his associations with The Rolling Stones and Sex Pistols, got some great Mondays quotes out of the band. It was Stone Roses' drummer Reni who prompted Bez to give one of the best of all drug quotes by noting that the errant dancer had, the previous night, set light to his bed. "There were flames coming from his pillow, and 'e didn't know nowt about it...'e was fucking comatose."

Bez's reaction? (without a hint of irony): "Aye, when your bed's on fire you know you're dealing with top fucking draw."

Top Of The Pops danced to a different drum that night, as the surly, gate-crashing Mondays and Stone Roses draped themselves over the furniture and gloated in the music press attention. As though trying to pull at a teenage suburban party, they intimidated as many as they drew towards them, two bands hot to trot and without a care in the world.

Roses singer Ian Brown: "The Roses and the Mondays have the same influences really: blues clubs, reggae nights, a bit of Parliament, a bit of Funkadelic...we're taking it from the same record collections, just doin' it up different."

"The only rivalry between us and The Roses has been a bit of a race to see who has got the flashiest clothes, right, and what part of the world these clothes come from, 'cos we're both flash cunts, knowaarraamean?" added Ryder. "They are dead brilliant, The Roses. They are more tuneful than us, but we are a top band too so it works great together. I reckon, I mean, I call 'em mates: Ian, fuckin' Mani, Reni - friends. And particularly Cressa - man, wharrayy - we taught him everything he fuckin' knows."

Two bands, a little sliver of pop history, mimed their way to a first peak for Madchester together that night. "Do you think my willy will look big enough hangin' in these fuckin' strides?" Ryder asked the make-up girl.

"To be honest" said Bez, a day after the show, "It were a good laugh to see 'em all. If all goes well, we may not see them for another five years...I reckon they'll be bigger than us. Pompous superstars and all that. Great lads, but when it gets that big who knows how it will change. It would fuckin' change me, that's for sure."

Glory days, but for some the beginning of the end. A great part of Manchester felt that Madchester died the moment the two bands hit the *Top Of The Pops* stage. The moment had gone, the scene evaporated - from then on, instead of belonging to them, Madchester belonged to the world, like Coca Cola, Ford or Kodak. Every pop movement experiences the same moment - rock 'n' roll, Merseybeat, punk, new wave and so on. For early fans of the Mondays, the band were slipping into the mainstream, and their music was missing from the more sussed Manchester dance floors after that night. In a sense they were right. That first, fresh scene around the Mondays had indeed died.

"Our real friends were not in the least bit bothered about us going on *Top Of The Pops*," growled Shaun Ryder, "in fact they were fucking well made up. It was all those fuckin' trendy types, the floppy fucking students. They were the ones saying, "Oh, I don't like them anymore, they have gone on *Top Of The Pops*." Fucking cunts. All of them. They were never real fans. It's like, over in England, when someone gets a nice car and some bastards smash it up because they haven't got one. Shitpots. It's just daft. They never had a real life, them idiots. I never wanted them near the band in the first place, jumped-up tossers living in a dream world. This is for real for us. It's our only fucking way out, isn't it? I'm sorry for the people who are still stuck in the shit but I can hardly take the whole of fucking working class Salford with me, can I? They should cherish the success. That's what it has always been about. Not some fucking trendy, studenty, hippy idea that we shouldn't sell out. Fuck. I thought we were past all that. The whole point is to sell out or else fuck off and let someone else have a bash."

Shaun also said at the time: "It was when I got to thirty, I knew I would have to calm down a bit. Didn't want to end up like an old alkie with me drugs. It freaked me out big time. You do get wiser. When you are young, you have got your own opinion too. If there's a question for me now, I'm like a computer. I go, "Brain, give me five possible solutions to this problem." I now see things in 3D."

1990

The peak year of Madchester was the most tumultuous year in the Happy Mondays collective life. Things began weirdly, and soon became weirder still. This probably explains why, to this day, Shaun Ryder prefers to retreat to his stock answer, whenever asked questions about the Mondays so-called golden years: "Fuck me, 1990, I can 'ardly remember a thing. Can't remember that fuckin' Wembley Arena gig. Know we did it, read reviews an' that, but that year...when was it? 1990, more than a blur, mate...wiped out really." This 'erased' period began rather well, when on January 10th, and much to the chagrin of the tabloid gossip hacks, Shaun Ryder was finally acquitted, by Jersey magistrates of the importation and possession of cocaine. This potentially serious charge was the residual effect of Ryder's aforementioned Jersey meeting with Karl Denver. At the Customs point, seven thousandths of a gramme of cocaine were found to be lurking deeply within Shaun's pockets. Even the most moralistic of Jersey magistrates noted that it wasn't particularly unusual for a rock star to be in possession of cocaine, and that it would be most unusual if that minuscule quantity had been brought onto the island with a view to re-sale.

He's Gonna Step On You

In February, the band were invited to pluck a song from the

disparate, and largely rather inspiring Elektra Records back catalogue for the label's 40th anniversary album *Rubaiyat*. Initially, being hearty fans of the mighty Tom Waits - in particular, his Elektra Years compilation album - the Mondays were going to take on the gargantuan task of recording one of his songs. Ryder: "We thought about Waits' stuff, it would have been really cool but then someone, can't think who it was, came up with this John Kongos song. I vaguely remember it from being like dead young and it being on the radio. But it was great. We knew it would be great." In fact, the John Kongos song, 'He's Gonna Step On You Again', had been a mere afterthought, slapped onto the back of a tape full of Tom Waits and Doors songs, sent over from Elektra. It wasn't, after all, regarded as one of the label's finer achievements.

In essence, the band jumped straight into the song. It was a wholly natural affair, punching out its more obvious popisms and rendering it part of the whole, part of the Mondays groove. Nathan McGough: "We always seemed to know that it would be really big. I think, probably, it was Rowetta's backing vocals that convinced us. Fantastic, man. Couldn't believe it when I first heard the tape. What a groove. It was just pure Mondays and, if it goes down in history as their finest moment - although the band would all seem to plum for the mighty Paul Oakenfold re-mix of 'Wrote For Luck' - as their track, then no-one would object. It just worked." It worked so well, in fact, that 'Step On' was duly claimed by the band for a single, which reached No. 5 in the UK singles chart, forcing them to record a parallel version of Kongos' other British hit, 'Tokoloshe Man', for the Elektra album. Though a sprightly attempt, and a recording which holds its own on the Mondays end of career compilation album *Loads*, it failed to capture the same magic, the same easy flow funk. 'Step On' seemed simple, perfect, natural and fresh. By comparison 'Tokoloshe Man' was rather laboured. Nevertheless, the choice of Kongos, though little more than a fluke, was rather inspired. Originally, the songs had brightened up a British singles chart, and a British rock scene that had been suffocating beneath appalling extremes - the daft pop end of glam rock and the dull groan of the profoundly anti-single, progressive rock scene. Although no-one knew the slightest thing about Kongos, his ability to come up with singles that appealed to both extremes was worthy of considerable praise.

A body, a street, a gig

The body was in the street, in the middle of the street. Lying stock still. A car cruised to a halt. Two people, curious or frightened, stepped out and took a long look at the body before getting back in and driving off, down through the enveloping shadows of Manchester's evocative Little Peter Street. There seemed to be no life in the body at all until, after the first few drops of rain had splashed on the forehead, and after the clothes had soaked in enough moisture to signal some kind of instinctive panic, the eyes opened, the head rolled weirdly to one side until the eyes focused on the red outside door of The Boardwalk. Bez was in the street again, blurry eyed and dreamy. Through his misty vision he saw two figures walking slowly towards him. Recognising one of them to be Boardwalk owner Colin Sinclair, he smiled...all would be well.

Colin Sinclair: "It wasn't the first time. It had happened before - I remember finding him in the street. We lifted him up and brought him back inside The Boardwalk, where we gave him some coffee and tried to figure out where he was meant to be and what he was meant to be doing. He kept muttering something about a gig, so we rang Tracey at Factory to find out. It turned out he was supposed to be gigging that night in Newcastle. So Tracey eventually arranged to fly him up there. We took him to the airport, dropped him off and, literally shoved him on the plane. Apparently someone at the other end grabbed him and took him to the gig. I don't think, to this day, that he has a clue how he got from the gutter to the stage. He just woke up and he was playing bongos."

In truth, Bez wouldn't have been so worried - he had been

shunted through a rock and roll lifestyle for two whole years. And that little incident was a perfect microcosm of Bez's entire career. From the gutter to the stage, dreamily. Bez in a nutshell. This Newcastle date was also non-memorable for Shaun Ryder: "It happened to me a lot, not knowing where I was, I tell you, those Wembley Arena dates. I know we played them. I've seen the reviews, but I can't remember a single thing about any of them. And at Newcastle, well, I was late for that Newcastle gig, very late. So I gets there and all these security guards are giving me double hassle and I just couldn't understand it. I kept saying, "Let me through you bastards, I'm the lead singer." They looked a bit dubious for a while, nodding to each other, like, before they all seem to agree and began clearing a way for me to get to the stage. Right down to the front they took me. I climbed on and I remember feeling really shocked. The place looked so plush and massive. All posh seats and that. Then it dawned on me that I wasn't at our gig at all. I was in Simply Red's venue down the road."

*   *   *

Shaun Ryder. "Bez wrote three cars off in three weeks. We keep lending him cars, man, and he keeps writing them off. Honda Prelude, Golf GTI...and he's not even passed his test."

*   *   *

Wander into The Boardwalk and glance inside the Happy Mondays rehearsal room. In the same little complex that would later produce Oasis and, at that time housed The Fall, The Stone Roses et al. All rehearsal rooms, when occupied by a band, look the same, don't they? A disgusting mess of crushed beer cans, overflowing ash trays, chip papers, fag packets, the obligatory coffee cups brimming with fungi, a spaghetti mesh of twisted wires on the floor, the eerie silence of abandoned guitars. And would the rehearsal room used by Happy Mondays be any different? Any more disgusting than that?

Well, consider the task facing The Boardwalk team when, following the departure of the Mondays, they attempted to prize their way into the said rehearsal room. What dark horrors awaited them. Piles of vomit. Urine stained corners. Pyramid stacks of a dubious and unidentifiable nature. You think I'm exaggerating? Happy Mondays chalked a new practice room low at The Boardwalk, a depravity that far outstrips anything that might appear in any Spinal Tap parody. Their practice room remains, to this day, the only room at The Boardwalk, and possibly in the whole of rock that necessitated the calling in of the city council sanitation department. Sinclair and staff, although strangely reluctant to relive this moment of horror, have confirmed that it is, indeed, a true story.

CHAPTER 12

March 1990

Art is Spain. There were many occasions when Happy Mondays deemed it necessary to 'Salfordise' a studio or, for that matter, a hotel room, or a hotel, or a bar, a venue or, a town. This is exactly the effect they achieved within seconds of arriving at Barcelona's ARS Studio, in March 1990. They stumbled into its pristine black and chromed perfection like a marauding army, instantly draping over the pear-shaped bar, devouring huge sandwiches ("Fuckin' 'ell man, it's like an elephant's dick, this one"), gorging, drinking and, of course, skinning up. The ritual was rounded off as the atmosphere in the room changed, as the atmosphere in all Happy Mondays recreational rooms would change, from bright and sparkly to a foggy hue, complete with wave upon wave of eerie smoke circulating above them, before drifting out through the air vents. Happy Mondays had landed, surprisingly mellow after several brushes with the heavily armed Spanish law and a couple of blown out tour dates. Such, for a while, was life.

They disembarked from a coach which had rumbled for six hours across Spain, stopping off at Stiges, the place often referred to as the 'gay capital of Europe'. Once deposited in that most unlikely town, Happy Mondays naturally, fell into a state of rampage. In one particular club, rather meekly called Ricky's, the band romped around the bar, making heady fun of the locals, as Gaz put it: "fuckin' shirt-lifters of Faggotsville. We watched them stuffing their hands down each others trousers and slapping each other on the bum. We 'ad a right laugh, though it got a bit 'eavy at one point when some of 'em - big 'uns, too - began to seriously object. Can't think what upset them. No sense of humour, or what?"

Not everyone in the Mondays entourage was 'Happy'. It is interesting to note these words, relayed later in the *NME*, from their coach driver Basil: "I've done lots of tours with American bands in Europe. They all like a puff. But they are all so paranoid they almost eat the roaches afterwards. But Happy Mondays don't seem to give a fuck. One of the bastards broke a key in the door lock to the coach last night. I'll get them back now. I'll frighten the fuck out of them on this next bit." Basil would later disappear from the band's life in Amsterdam, completely and instantly, after having his beer heavily spiked with acid.

Having expertly extracted themselves from the firm grip of the resultant officers of the law, Happy Mondays carried a 're-styling' of Barcelona's premier television studio. Not for the first time on their European tour, they would defy belief before a barrage of cameras. Unusually, however, the gleaming misfortunates who had been forced to conduct the interview did, at least, understand a little about what it was that made the Monday's tick. The interview in question would be relayed later to the British public via the pages of the *NME*. And what fun it was.

Question: "What is Happy Mondays?"
Shaun: "Dunno. I haven't worked that one out yet. Probably something suitable for Club 18-30'ers."
So where would Happy Mondays be without Ecstacy? (Good question):
Shaun: "Much richer."
You've spent eight years together as a band. How have you managed to achieve this?
Gaz: "By being heavily sedated."
Shaun: "I don't like talking. I can't since I cut me hair."
Have the music press been useful to building you up in England?
Shaun: "Yeah, they like us because we give them drugs."
So what is the Mondays philosophy?
Gaz: "To have a good time, all the time."
Excuse me. Our TV programme is called Sputnik. Could you say something about Sputnik...I like Sputnik because....
(Shaun, unlike the Spanish interviewers, was more than aware

that Sputnik in Madchester and possibly nowhere else, was a harsh and head blowing form of dope).
Shaun: "Well, what can I say about it?"
Gaz: "How about, give us a quarter."
Shaun: "No..no..give us an ounce."
Gaz: "Do you want brown or black?"

Needless to say, the Spanish interviewers, and, indeed, the cameramen, technicians, gophers, directors and, probably the tea ladies as well, all stood in stony silence, attempting to make sense of this little word interplay which would have been surreal had it appeared on English TV., But to the Spaniards, unsure of their references, it must have been both wholly incomprehensible and utterly impossible to counter.

"It's always like that," Shaun remarked afterwards "because, we have found out nobody else quite lives in the same world as us. Those Spanish TV people were alright, but we can't go all bright and smiley, and be dead nice 'cos it just wouldn't be natural. So we live in our own little world and these media people just have to take what they can and make of it...well, what do they make of it all? I've no idea. It's all mad, ain't it."

The British tabloid gossip columns, having discovered and devoured the Mondays on several occasions, were suspiciously alerted and suitably delighted the next day when photographs of Ryder would appear next to the extremely newsworthy fallen idol of Coronation Street, Nigel Pivaro, aka the dreadful, snivelling, womanising Terry Duckworth. He appeared, video camera welded to his arm, in a number of photographs with Shaun. To the band, this wasn't such an unlikely occurrence as Pivaro had been an old school chum of both the Ryder's. What, was perhaps a mite surprising was Pivaro's tentish flares, a full-sailed and rather corny vision of Madchester that even the most naive and exploitable schoolboy would reject if he found them languishing cheaply on a market stall. Pivaro, contrary to the tabloid headlines that depicted him as a washed-out, penniless has-been, had actually been holidaying along the coast and simply decided to spend some time with his mates. As it turned out, he appeared in the middle of a typically and hilariously volatile soundcheck.

Things had started meekly enough, with Derek Ryder grasping a bass guitar and, goaded by Shaun, attempting a particularly dashing impression of New Order's Hooky, legs spread to a V, bass touching the floor, complete with Joy Division bass line booming eerily through the speakers. It was this outburst that kicked off the trouble, because before the band were two numbers into their soundcheck, the Spanish police made an unwelcome invasion. Upon seeing the cops entering the club, various members of the band's twenty strong entourage were seen running suspiciously into the shadows, and sliding through the exit doors. It was a bust. Accusing eyes flashed everywhere, Bez flounced into the dressing room, his arm wrapped around some kind of package. Derek Ryder began to affect an "I'm just the roadie here, man" aloof whistle while the club manager, a first class turncoat bastard of the slimiest variety, immediately fell onto the side of the cops. The police, noisy, aggressive, pushy and arrogant, seemed to have a strange effect on this character who soon began to nod in vacuous agreement. As it turned out, the cops were merely attempting to keep the band's noise to a minimum. This fact angered McGough, who immediately flew into attack mode, although the incident soon washed over the strangely relieved members of the band. Quietly, they returned to the stage and plunged through 'Wrote For Luck'. "Nowt ta worry about," said Shaun "they weren't interested in drugs after all."

This wasn't strictly true. At the close of the Mondays' set that night, the band returned to their dressing room to find two plain clothes policemen rifling through their bags and coats. Within seconds of leaving the stage, the entire Happy Mondays entourage had left the building, filtering out into the Barcelona night, seeking safety and replacement chemicals: "At least the filth got sorted for the weekend," stated a sardonic Nathan McGough.

*   *   *

Tony Wilson: "I once called them scum. They protested. They said "Tony, we are not scum." But I said, "Listen, last week Shaun was attempting to find his way back to a studio. Then he said, 'Oh, it must be this way...there's Bez's sick on the pavement. Now if that isn't scum, I don't know what is."

*   *   *

Shaun Ryder: "I've stopped taking E. Last time I did, I was the last one out of the warehouse. Didn't know where I was. I had a load of E in my pockets 'cos I was selling them. I put about ten in my mouth to go out and they all melted. Sent me potty and I ended up having a heart attack on the Oxford Road, collapsing and ending up in BUPA. Took me three weeks to recover. I couldn't even move the side of me body. Totally cabbaged."

Totally cabbaged, too, in the Moon Club in Reykjavik, where the band performed in front of a wild and shambolic audience comprising of local sweaty fat men. The crowd had drunk themselves into their usual Friday night stupor and, as seems the habit in Iceland, felt that bashing everyone else's brains in would make a fitting climax to the evening. Perhaps it would have been acceptable had they bashed each others brains in but, instead, they turned to Manc contingent and the 100 strong mob from London's Brain Club for their sport. Perhaps the locals had been incensed by the sight of Derek Ryder donning a Viking Norseman helmet and dancing away on the disco columns. Earlier Derek had grabbed his private parts and screamed to a photographer "Get a shot of this, 'ere, this is where the Mondays began." Three of the heavyweight locals, apparently incensed by Shaun's swearing, leapt onto Bez on the post-gig dance floor, intent on thoroughly sorting out this manic Manc. Luckily for Bez, one of the London mob - an acid Ted - ploughed in and single-handedly reduced the locals to jibbering wrecks. It wasn't the most pleasant of gigs. Nor was it the most pleasant of plane rides home either, as Shaun Ryder found himself constantly pestered by a wayward fan who had, as fans sometimes do, expected Ryder to be brimming with gentle, welcoming bonhomie, accepting him into the circle. The fan soon turned nasty and chose to ignore Ryder pleas to "go fuck yourself." A scuffle burst out, 1000 feet over Iceland, which resulted in Happy Mondays roadie Muzzer, spurred on by chants of "Goooo ooon Muzzzer, smack 'im," head-butting the unfortunate assailant. The incident was serious enough to almost cause a forced landing in Glasgow.

March 24th and 25th, 1990, G-Mex parties

Two sell out dates at G-Mex. Parallel raves, each attracting 9,000 Mondays addicts. Mostly, it seemed, the same 9,000 Mondays addicts, just getting into their second wind for the following day. It came quicker than expected, as Madchester exploded out of all proportion. Just fifteen months previously, the Mondays had provided a spirited support set to New Order, who hadn't sold out, at the same venue. Back then, with Madchester just another prospective Factory marketing ploy, Shaun Ryder had drifted sullenly off the stage before uttering, "Fucking cold dump...fucking shed...how are you supposed to whip up an atmosphere in a dump like this?" This hadn't been mere frustration, or even sour grapes, for ever since its initial conversion from the rotting shell of Central Station into G-Mex, the venue had always been a notoriously poor rock gig, blessed with all the acoustic possibilities and ambience of a roofless farmyard barn. Even The Smiths, at their very peak, during the Festival Of The Tenth Summer in '86, had failed to break the venue's deadening calm. Mostly, it was only really good for fat, lazy stadium acts - Chris Rea, Spandau Ballet et al. That gig was arguably one of the Mondays worst. Ironically, Ryder's frustration proved unwarranted. The Mondays actually stole the day.

The portents, however, hadn't really been in place. Nobody

from or around the Mondays camp really expected the band to fill G-Mex twice by March 1990. When Nathan McGough initially approached the band with the idea for the dates, he had received a firm rebuff. The truth was that nobody genuinely believed that they could sell the tickets. Shaun Ryder: "It just seemed like a load of hassle, the very idea of headlining in a place like that seemed, well, it seemed too much like hard work. All of us gathered around and agreed - fucking hell, it would have to be like playing a small club, wouldn't it - we could get on, bash about for half an hour and fuck off and have a good time. That was always the Mondays way, never ones to work ourselves into the ground. But G-Mex...Jeezus...we weren't U2 and we knew it."

Eventually, while ignoring the pleas from the 'business heads' at Factory, the band decided to go ahead with the dates on the advice of two of the local lads who handled their merchandising, Jimmy and Muffy. Being bona fide Mancs and great friends who were close to the heart of the band, they wielded more power over the Mondays than any music business bods. Their advice to the Mondays was: "Do it lads, we'll sell it for you, do it..be a gas..no probs, lads, we'll get it sorted."

The Mondays weren't U2, indeed, but the G-Mex dates, as they turned out, weren't really rock gigs at all. They were gatherings, raves, punched along by the hallowed sounds of DJ Paul Oakenfold and supported by the ambience of 808 State. In a sense, the Mondays came and went as a mere side attraction. Their set was (as captured somewhat inelegantly on film for 'Rave On - The Video') a triumph, a band finally reaching the peak of their own particularly surreal mountain. Admittedly, also a band looking exhausted, spent, but at the same time wearily ecstatic. The truth was that, at the heart of the 9,000 attendees, 400 or so were the band's closest friends - a sizeable chunk of Salford youth - who formed a hard core inner circle. This was the Mondays, expanded for two nights. No, not like U2. Unlike any other band on Earth.

CHAPTER 13

Spring 1990. Parisian chic. Bobbed hair and fake fur. Little heart-shaped faces and ankle boots. Fringes and swimming pool eyes. Shopping. Paris in 1990 and the Arndale Centre back home seemed worlds apart, but the Mondays and their mates - wolf-whistling and bawdy - made for a pretty common factor. Who were these vacuous people? Football supporters? The chic Parisian youth gasped in disbelief at this strange little invasion, all hooded tops, baggy denims and floppy white cotton T-shirts. Skunk and beer, E and Orangina. Psychedelia.

The E generation had come by ferry, by coach and by car, perhaps abroad for the first time, out of it. Dancing down the Champs Elysees, bouncing over Renaults and Peugeots, rolling through Pigale like naughty school kids away from the teacher. Rushing into clubs and dancing like no-one had danced in France before.

Bohemian Paris was once again changed by an influx from outside. The Mondays came to town, but more importantly for the Parisian kids from the suburbs, the Mondays fans came with them, so the whole culture was in evidence, not just its leaders. It was a wild, hedonistic, youthful mingling, almost without violence. Manc lads and Parisian girls, Mondays girls and les garcons de Paris, the sixty hour round trip washed through the town and was gone. Peppered with music hacks, some along for the ride, some brought by Factory specifically, it was a party of the highest order. I remember seeing *NME* writer Sarah Champion face down in the street somewhere around the Ecole Militaire. The fact that I can't remember a lot more than that is testament to how great a time we had. More than ever, the notion that the Mondays had 'fans' was dispelled. The Stone Roses had fans but the Mondays were simply at the centre of a major party, and for the Paris trip the whole party came along. The fact that the band stumbled along with everyone else made the point clearer.

Chris Heath, writing for *The Face*, tried to catch the whole reasoning: "They like the fact the Mondays are working class lads who couldn't give a shit about anything. They think the Mondays are laughing all the way to the bank and to the next drugs stash - "They are on a good thing and they know it," - they are just normal."

From what I saw of the event, it was first and foremost a big piss-up as far as most of the revellers were concerned. Being in a club. Happy. Sneaking acid out of the country! A thousand Mancs and pseudo-Mancs crammed into the Bataclan, facing the wrong way to dance, cheering at the wrong time for the music but the right time for the moment, scuffling, bobbing about, screaming and falling over. Grab a stranger and see what happens...It was just like The Hacienda!

That afternoon, Shaun Ryder had been out on the streets, drifting merrily from cafe to cafe, unusually non the worse for drink, happy just to soak in the Parisian atmosphere. "Shaun was almost embarrassed," stated a member of the Burnley posse, "he just sat at the back of the bar, being reet polite, like, smokin' a bit and sippin' beer. It was almost mellow."

Later in the afternoon, he was curled up next to his girlfriend Trisha, dispensing wisecracks left and right. "Nathan, go an' get me a fuckin' ghetto blaster, it's so fuckin' dead in 'ere. The party's out on the fuckin' streets man. Typically, and I have to say this happens a lot, we find ourselves locked in some fucking crap-hole of a dressing room while the fans are out there having a fucking ball. Did that ever happen to the fucking Rolling Stones? Like fuck it did? Jeeez, Nath, it says here that we are on for two hours. Jeez, man, I didn't do two hours for my holy communion."

Ten minutes later and the band were into a soundcheck far more entertaining that the set itself, including a hilarious version of the Olivia Newton John/John Travolta hit 'Summer Nights, complete with wah-wah guitar. A tremendous version of 'He's Gonna Step On You Again' with Rowetta on backing vocals saw Ryder insert whatever ad libs he could pluck from his dark and vulgar muse into the song's vast open spaces, most notably perhaps switching the famous "melon twisting" line to "Yer fuckin' round in Paris, man.'"

After the soundcheck, Shaun Ryder wandered to the middle of the Bataclan auditorium, peeling himself away from the clutches of McGough who, in turn was attempting to fend off twelve leather-jacketed French rock journalists, all of whom appeared to be labouring under the impression that they had been promised 'exclusives'. Ryder told a startled Chris Heath from Q magazine that, if he wanted some kind of interview, he would have to do it then and there, as the fans began to pour into the hall - many of them attempting, and the prettier one's succeeding, in poncing French currency off their hero. It was an interesting moment with Ryder, for once free from the inner circle of his friends, and thoroughly slagged by the rapidly increasing swell around him: "Yer a fucking cunt, yer are Ryder," one of them playfully and eloquently informed him. The retort from the singer was a swift and not too gentle, rabbit punch. The post-gig party, at a gay club called La Luna, was attended by hundreds, although most seemed content to spill around the sidewalk, waiting patiently for their allotted coach drivers to assert their authority and call the whole thing to a halt.

Chris Heath later recalled the scene on one particular coach returning to Doncaster: "The Donnie Posse fondly recall their days antics. They've puked in pubs, they've been ripped off by taxi drivers (£20 for a few hundred yards), a hamburger stall (£9 for a hot dog) and a street salesman, (£9 for a belt they thought was 60p). "We haven't got a centime left." In the hotel they bust the toilet seat, used a chair in the shower and squirted the shower hose out the window. They are thrilled because Shaun shouted "Doncaster" on stage. "I drunk from Bez's water bottle," says one. Another trumps in, "I gave Bez some tobacco for his spliff."

Mellow Yellow

Donovan Leitch came into the Happy Mondays family, not

through a spliffed-out rendezvous in Laurel Canyon, or a mantra-driven session on a Greek island, but in the grey and un-romantic town of Colne in Lancashire. Donovan was gigging locally, still playing the wonderfully simple and essential hits of his sixties heyday, sprinkled with later songs that few knew but many enjoyed.

On the surface the two musical camps were worlds apart. Mondays, fuelled by E and angst through years of criminal and anti-social behaviour, with little to endear them to the world at large. Donovan, a middle-aged man, remembered fondly by a generation for being the proto-typical pace and love provider, a veteran of The Beatles sojourn in India with the much-famed Maharishi, and the 'All You Need Is Love' session, gently spoken and softly singing.

Donovan himself, however, was more aware of their similarities. Noting the increasing resurgence of sixties psychedelia in the current scene, he was aware of the influence there: "I've been aware that there is a Manchester happening going on...and have been to a few house clubs...a lot of the Manchester scene is emulating my own stuff."

The Mondays hatched a plot to kidnap the old troubadour and invite him along on tour as special guest. Unable to make it immediately, Donovan - far more adventurous both musically and in life than his reputation might have implied - was definitely up for it: "It's going to be a good vibe at the Mondays shows. I'm looking forward to them tremendously," he ventured, "a lot of the audiences are like the early Donovan audiences, who were very much into trance and dance."

Ryder: "Well, we've always been into that. Especially when all the E came along, especially in Ibiza, at three in the morning when all the mellow times come on and it was double mellow E and all that. Donovan - mellow, mellow man, just sitting there, soaking it all in, very nineties, very sixties. Same fucking thing, man. 'Course, we are into Donovan...why does that surprise people?"

Sometimes derided for hippy-trippy nonsense, Donovan was in fact always a serious-minded writer, with a wonderful ear for melody - often very simply conceived melody, with a rich vocal delivery. His work went far beyond the hit singles remembered by Radio 2 audiences, and for those fans of his who saw his light shining again through the Mondays influence, it was a heart-warming time. It was good to see teenage kids dancing to his largely acoustic songs, and amusing to see the old heads as they tried to figure out whether these kids were genuinely interested or simply taking the piss.

Glastonbury 1990

From its earliest days, Glastonbury has had a reputation for capturing bands at their peak, and wringing the very best from them. From hippy to baggy, from Rollins to Pulp, the festival has escaped PR nightmares, greying hippiedom and legendary mud, to emerge in the nineties as hip and fun. Over the years, Glastonbury stood tall against the punk invasion, but gradually shook off its image of turgid guitar onanists and 'real music' and finally 'got real' itself. In 1990, Salford moved south and the Glastonbury Festival surrendered to baggy.

One Mondays follower, Harry, summed it up: "I'd never seen anything like it, all of Manchester seemed to be there, people I'd not seen for years. Like all the folk who'd go to all the different clubs in town would suddenly be together, romping in the mud. It was unbelievable, they...we...totally took over the place." Happy Mondays took their party to Glastonbury. They weren't entirely welcomed and stretched the naturally tolerant nature of the festival to the max, ripping down the barriers to the backstage area, pulling their friends into the fray, partying like crazy yet eventually producing a live set that was regarded as their finest ever. Once again, Glastonbury had unwittingly produced the best. The media flocked to the Mondays set - *NME* alone sent at least twenty writers, all swapping their regulation issue black Levis for 'trendy' shorts. Mark E Smith looked on in disdain: "You could tell the fuckers a mile away...oh, how could they lower themselves?"

It wasn't just shorts, it was sunglasses also. All twenty journalists were sunglassed and shorted, claiming that the sunglasses were purely practical, to shield their eyes from the sun. Happy Mondays soon requested that the sunglasses be removed. "You are freaking the band out," a security guard told the startled hacks, "they think you are all drug squad."

It was a great day. Paradoxically, it has been argued it was also the day that marked the beginning of the end for Madchester, and perhaps for the Mondays. The biggest party precedes the biggest comedown and, after everyone had departed, leaving little but an empty bowl crammed with beer cans and crisp packets, something seemed to have been lost. How anti climactic. How could it be like that ever again?

In fact, the change began not after, but during Glastonbury. Until that point, the whole of the British music press and the Happy Mondays following had been sharing the joke with Shaun. They had been part of the joke, part of the party. It had been a scream. But suddenly there was a subtle twist. That little episode with the sunglasses, perhaps, provided a hint. Rumour had it that Happy Mondays had taken it too far. That they had tilted over the edge. That they had edged into paranoia. Oh, it was okay for all those little student bods to join the party, mess with a little acid, or whatever, but eventually they would leave, and trip back to their middle class homes and jobs and families. At some point, the Mondays would have to branch off from them, go it alone again. The source of that split could be traced to that monumental Glastonbury appearance. People were no longer laughing with Shaun Ryder...they were laughing at him. More specifically, at his antics. but also at his problems too. And they were laughing at Bez. And Nathan. And the rest. It was rumoured that the heavily sedated Shaun Ryder had pissed his pants, that he was totally out of control. People laughed at that. They wanted a freak show.

Worse still, people started scrutinising the records as well as the lifestyle. They felt these records that had been glued to their record decks, that had sound-tracked one of the most fascinating musical eras in rock history, weren't strictly too good. Happy Mondays won a mighty victory at Glastonbury but, ultimately they sowed the seed for their eventual destruction. People stopped believing. People moved on. Left the party. Went on to the next stage of their life adventure. Immediately, Madchester had greyed into nostalgia.

CHAPTER 14

Mondays in Manhattan

For many bands, the peak moment in their early career tends, comes not with the initial thrill of *Top Of The Pops* nor, indeed, their first sell-out gig in their home town. It is the first time a car picks them up from John F Kennedy Airport and whisks them straight into the crazy huddle of giant rectangular monsters that is Manhattan. Whether sliding through snow-lined freeways or cowering beneath the heat of the city's strangulating summer, no band can fail to feel the thrill. If you can make it there...

There is a great photo of the Mondays taken by Kevin Cummins, their old Salford confidante. Frolicsome, ragged, cheeky and Mancunian to a fault, the band are dwarfed by the twin towers of the Word Trade Centre behind them, its disapproving stare seeming to ask on behalf of the whole Big Apple "Who the fuck are these guys?"

Where most bands are taken by the hand and led through the mid-town shopping districts, discos and donut joints by their American record company executives, the Monday chose to go it alone and consequently got held up at gun-point in Harlem. Not satisfied with viewing the city from a gentle, touristic platform at skyscraper level, the Mondays headed defiantly beyond that point where the taxi drivers say "No", and found themselves in one of the toughest districts of Harlem, looking of course, for more rocks to keep the party moving. Drifting through these streets looking for a fix is probably an activity that even the craziest head would deem naive, or downright stupid, but Shaun and Bez disappeared into the shadows as though this was their second home, relying on new-found friends to make connections on street corners. Shaun later described the dealers, users and pushers as "rocked up to fuck". While he rocked from foot to foot, waiting to score, Bez started frothing at the mouth and spitting. This was enough for one of the dealers to pull a gun on them.

Shaun: "I'm standing there with a bottle of Budweiser in my hand...I'm just gonna put the bottle in his face 'cos I'm high on crack and don't give a fuck about no gun..." In the nick of time, before the trigger finger could squeeze, the Mondays' new friends appeared to cool the situation. Either way, a murder rap or being shot themselves, the lads were out of it. Shaun: "I was a bit startled, though, when I thought about it afterwards and realised that nobody seemed particularly concerned...it ain't got that bad in Manchester, yet, but, well...it could be going that way." And how did Bez sum the trip up? "Well er, Manhatten? We hung around in a park, smokin' stuff...with some black geezers, like."

November 17 1990

During the week running up to the release of *Pills, Thrills And Bellyaches*, advance orders for the album topped 150,000, immediately making it certain to eclipse anything the Mondays had previously recorded. Factory, partly in response to this demand, set about orchestrating a new distribution set up throughout Europe for the album. It was a simple case of synergy, the result of Wilson receiving a barrage of business truths from Roger Ames at London Records. Previously, Factory had dealt with a bewilderingly complex proliferation of differing, and sometime opposing, European labels. This time, urged on by the disarmingly clever McGough, Factory would use a single label approach for the release. Factory's Paul Cons stated: "Our approach towards international sales is under constant review and the move underlines Factory's ability to adopt different promoters, marketing and distribution systems as they suit our needs. The release of the Monday's album will help us evaluate the potential of the various international systems available."

Pills, Thrills and Bellyaches

Derek Ryder: "Oh yeah, *Pills, Thrills And Bellyaches*, our so-called "difficult third album". Nobody thought that the Mondays would be able to do anything after *Bummed*. They thought "Yeah, it was a good time, but that's it, the third album will be a stinker. It always is. Well with Happy Mondays it fucking wasn't, was it? *Pills* was an all time classic. So there you are."

Until Happy Mondays skipped naturally into the wholly refreshing *Pills, Thrills and Bellyaches*, the notion of top DJ's evolving into top producers seemed, to say the least, unlikely. Effectively, however, Oakenfold and Osborne had been operating as producers for several years. Paul Oakenfold's previously praised re-mix of 'Wrote For Luck' was proof of this. Nathan McGough was the catalyst: "You should become producers," he stated simply, "beginning with our new album, it's gonna be some record."

Call that manager-speak if you like, but it really was some record. Recorded in the basement of Capital Tower, it oozes Mondays sunshine, reeks of the very heart of L.A. A near-perfect record, it was born out of frequent forays for the band along Hollywood and Sunset Boulevards, occasionally down to Pacific Palisades, the ocean and Malibu, or to the wonderful bohemia of Venice Beach. Ryder was at home with this bunch of weirdos.

Tony Wilson recalls flying to L.A. during the recording: "I arrived in L.A. at midnight, not a good time, really. I was all disorientated and numbed from the flight and buzzing a bit. So I checked in at my hotel and decided to drive over to the studio. There I was, going along Fountain Street. I can remember it as if it happened in slow motion, getting out of the car and walking down to the basement studios. It was so strange to see the band all sitting round, in that strangest of cities. And to my immense relief, they had obviously been working. A great noise was blasting out from underground and as I walked in Shaun was standing there and smiling and,

124

the music was 'Bob's Your Uncle'. They had just recorded it and it sounded absolutely fantastic. It was a real golden moment. I think I knew from then on, that *Pills* would be one of the great Factory albums...actually, one of the great British albums of the age."

In wandering straight into the middle of 'Bob's Yer Uncle', Wilson had stumbled across, arguably, the finest song the Mondays would ever record. Laid back and hearteningly rude, very L.A., it sounded like the Mama's And Papa's enjoying the kind of orgy one always hoped they would.

This was grubby, schoolboy Shaun, vocals way back in the mix, and rude - very rude. Oakenfold had suggested "C'mon, let's do a sexy one." Ryder, by his own admission couldn't write sensually. His take on writing sexual music was, in his words, to come up with "fuckin' pervy schoolboy stuff," and his clumsiness gives a frisson to the song which rolls and rolls along brilliantly.

'Loose Fit', meanwhile, Tony Wilson's favourite Mondays song, seemed like a rather obvious paean to 'baggy' at first, a simplistic statement about running around town and hanging loose. Perhaps it was, but it had been inspired, however distantly, by the Gulf War. Written while the Mondays were floating around America, their television viewing heavily punctuated by those oft-celebrated and despised CNN reports, piped directly to the band's hotel rooms. Ryder, slumped on numerous sofas, reeling from numerous spliffs, soaked in every broadcast, every missile crashing, every newshound ducking in the wake of a nearby explosion. The blurry fact-or-fiction TV became warped even further by the stunning brashness of the US channels. Hence, a bombing raid would be swiftly interrupted by 'Crazy Larry' trying to sell his dodgy cars. Bizarre...and Ryder loved every second. It was simply fantastic entertainment. Through Ryder's warped vision, everything twisted into 'Loose Fit'.

When the tapes finally arrived back at Factory, Wilson found it difficult to choose a single: "I argued a quite a bit with Nathan about that. I never thought that 'Kinky Afro' should be the first single. I knew that 'Loose Fit' was fantastic and instant and everything that a single should be, but not 'Kinky Afro', which I loved, absolutely, but not as a potential single. But I was wrong. It preceded the album and got to No. 5. My God, what a strange record to get into the top reaches of the chart. In my opinion...and I mean this, speaking, again, as an Oxbridge graduate rather than a record industry person, 'Kinky Afro' was the greatest poem about parenthood since 'Prayer For My Daughter'. Seriously, I believe it is great, great poetry, a stunning piece about a father imagining having a daughter and wondering what he would say to her. All that "I'm a scumbag, I'm gonna be a parent. What can I say? How can I live up to that?" What a heavy thought to put into just a pop record."

There was a little more to the 'Kinky Afro' cocktail than just that - Shaun's incredibly complex feelings towards his father are also in there. What was Derek doing as tour manager with the band? Was he stealing his son's thunder...living a life created by his son. The song is an exorcism, a way of pulling dark feelings out from within, and letting them go, a way of healing the relationship with his father rather than exposing the wounds. I don't know about Wilson's striking claims for Ryder's words, but there is no doubt that 'Kinky Afro', a paradoxically dark song on a light rollercoaster surf city album, contains a great deal of genuine emotion, however articulately, or inarticulately expressed.

Paul Ryder, of course, instantly recognised the references to Derek: "Shaun's words normally mean nothing to me," he stated, "except, sometimes, it'll be a bit personal towards someone and I'll tell him and he'll say "I didn't fucking mean that." But we both know that he did." Shaun meanwhile, would remain unmoved. "It's dead fucking tongue-in-cheek. When I wrote it, I got this song in me head by Hot Chocolate - 'Brother Louie' - and that's tongue-in-cheek so I wrote this the same." The infamous "Yippee Yippeee Aye Aye yahhhhh!" was, far from being enshrouded in mystery, simply stolen directly from Lady Marmalade. A clever little steal, actually, as the arrogance of the song, the solid, laddish brashness tends to prize your ears away from the original.

Wilson: "I don't think the Mondays would have been half as good had Ryder been fully educated - his words, they have a sharpness and a rhythm that would surely, have been battered out by a strong educational influence. Yes, these thoughts hit me after *Twenty Four Hour Party People* but I can't state this enough, he is one of the great modern poets." Shaun Ryder: "Oh, Tony's great, but he don't half talk a lot of bollocks sometimes. They are just jumbled words, maan, mostly don't mean fuck all."

There is an irony in Wilson's Oxbridge critique of Ryder's jumbled street words. Rock music in general, and Happy Mondays in particular, take words to the biggest possible audience in the shortest possible time. The problem is that this audience, once captured, will barely spend a moment analysing lyrics. Indeed, it has been proven many times that, although people may learn songs, word for word and often celebrate them as their favourites, so rarely do they spend time to examine, to *really* examine, the thoughts on offer. In any case, the Mondays, especially within the headier mixes of Oakenfold, are often quite impossible to decipher anyway, as the producer samples and twists Ryder's strikingly aloof tones, and filters them into the farthest corners of the mix.

Loose Fit, A Fashion Story: Gio Goi

"Here they come, sauntering down the street...La Coste on their chests, Reeboks on their feet..."

Happy Mondays were not so much clothes horses, but clothes donkeys. I mean this as a compliment. They were always the worst models in the world, and yet the best models in the world. Few bands had emerged in such gloriously unkempt glamour, such ragged sartorial honesty, such naturalness. This 'look' was so curiously subversive when seen on *Top Of The*

Pops (How they clashed with such neat, pristine little dancers, beaming careerist DJ's, and contrived glam popsters). It clearly contained a marketable power but, for so long, this remained invisible to the glossy fashion mags and the industry they serve. Here were a band who were dripping in up-to-the-minute street, club and school yard chic. A vision of council estate poise and suss. A band who could never bow to the whims of some idiotic Covent Garden-based fashion editor. In fashion terms, this was a different world, a real world. To his credit, Tony Wilson noticed this quite early and used a short feature on his own, local listings programme, *The Other Side Of Midnight*, to illustrate the point. As part of a short term, unofficial sponsorship deal, Wilson dragged the Mondays down to Shami Ahmed's streetwise 'Joe Bloggs' empire in Collyhurst, and filmed the band as they messed about, furiously trying on everything on the racks. It was a veritable orgy of 'baggy', and local Bloggs sales soared during the following week. This however, was merely a hint at what might be possible.

Something remarkable did happen. Something organic. Something straight from the Mondays inner circle, straight from the mouth of Shaun Ryder. Sitting around one night, soaking in the E, some sounds and a beer, Ryder began praising the entrepreneurial suss of two of his closest friends, the brothers Anthony and Chris Donnelly. "Why don't you design and make some clothes for us...for the band." he asked, before adding, "We'll all wear them, you know what we like to wear, you know what kids like. These fashion houses don't know shit, why not have a go?" What was to transpire was something of a triumph of talent, courage, endeavour and, of course, luck. Ryder had noticed the power and possibilities in two of his friends.

Anthony and Chris Donnelly, then 26 and 22 respectively, hailed from the vast Manchester overspill estate of Wythenshaw, an area, like much of Salford, simultaneously brimming with youthful talent and screaming decay. Sons of an Ardwick scrap metal merchant, and subsequently schooled

Happy Mondays, Salford Quays, early 1987

Shaun is famous for his photographic memory of lyrics

Derek, Shaun and Paul Ryder

The Reverend Black Grape

T In The Park, Glasgow, August 1995

Shaun Ryder, 1996

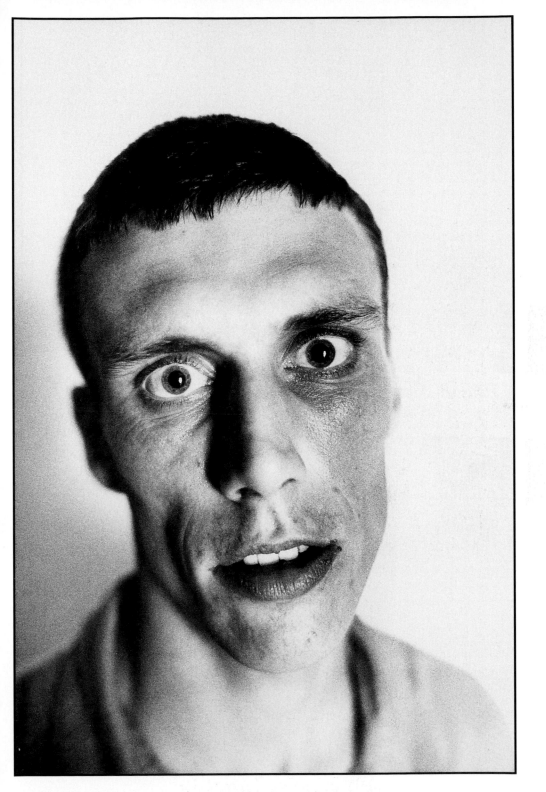

Bez...who else?

The oddest star of the nineties?

on the rules of the wilder side of life, the Donnellys first made their mark on the city's music scene by instigating a series of mid-eighties warehouse parties, self-explanatory dance nights that would eventually become known to the world as raves. They spent years dangerously perched on the tough, unofficial edge of the rock merchandising industry, selling posters, T-shirts and general streetwise ephemera. Unusually for merchandising pirates, the Donnellys soon built a reputation for selling only quality goods, a reputation so strong that a number of record companies, Factory among them, far from condemning them as pirates, actually enlisted their services. The Donnellys, like many kids in Manchester, had a talent that was simply waiting to explode. Ryder's encouraging words proved to be the impetus they needed. Their decision, that night, to take the fashion industry by storm might have seemed like mere drunken braggadocio. It was. Astonishingly, they succeeded.

Plucking a name straight out of a Vietnamese dictionary, Gio Goi (neither brother can remember quite what it means), they based their initial collection on just one T-shirt, sporting an Eagle logo on the front. Through the network of their friends, the legend of Gio Goi spread like wild-fire and, practically overnight, it became *de rigueur* on the city's nightclub scene. Suddenly, the marketing power - the power of the Mondays really - seemed so obvious. Gio Goi could supply genuine streetwise clothes - the fashion industry, not accustomed to being overtaken by a couple of mouthy northern brats, looked on in cynical disbelief. As the Gio Goi industry expanded, it was heavily rumoured that the heart of Gio Goi, far from being a slick marketing ploy, was locked in anarchic, unruly chaos. The rumour wasn't far from the truth. In fact it was rather worse than that.

"Their was one point," explains Anthony Donnelly, "when the entire fashion world seemed to be talking about us, and yet we were little more than a hired room in Ardwick and a couple of boxes of T-shirts and jeans. That was it. We really had to bluff our way through, but we did it because we didn't sell clothes, we sold attitude. Like the Mondays, we were and still are 100% Mancunian. Our clothes started to reflect the lifestyle of working class kids in Manchester, and everywhere else."

It was always a local thing. Anthony Donnelly further explains: "There was loads of, like, dead good looking birds on our estate so, we thought, we'd use them as models. Give 'em loads of free gear an' that. Keep 'em sweet. No point in going to model agencies an' all that crap." Gio Goi's true arrival on the fashion stage was announced, most spectacularly, at a fashion show in London. While all the other stands were immersed in the kind of white wine and gentle chit-chat that one might naturally associate with such an event, the Gio Goi stand exploded into a mini rave, complimented by no small number of inebriated, vulgar pop stars. Happy Mondays and The Stone Roses made appearances, and there were scores of dazed aggressive youths falling over and vomiting in the aisles. This scene was *Twenty Four Hour Party People* transposed into a fashion exhibit, and proved strangely attractive to the sycophantic vultures of the fashion industry, who suddenly wished to cash in on this natural state of anarchy. Much to the brothers surprise, the orders gushed in.

"It suddenly dawned on us," stated Chris, "that we would actually had to start doing some work. I had never done it before but, I thought, "Sod it, I'm a fashion designer." I began to scribble away. I knew nothin' about cloth or 'owt, but I knew what the kids wanted. Kids like me, really. I could see clearly where the fashion industry was going wrong. Absurdly enough, this was true. Chris's naive down-beat vision bridged the gap between the London-based fashion designer and the Manchester street brat with unnerving natural ease.

Today Gio Goi supply outlets across the world. "We are like pop stars in Japan," boasts Anthony. They own a small string of shops, with a show-piece Covent Garden establishment which opened in December 1994, a flourishing Salford gymnasium and a Cheshire farm retreat. It is here that, just occasionally, they invite their astonishingly disparate band of friends, from Wythensharian drop-outs to international fashion gurus, where they all have, in Chris's words, "a right good blast out. It were fucking great, the first one. Shaun came down and stayed in this little lodge we have at the gate, the neighbours couldn't fucking believe it."

Gio Goi...did that sound like free enterprise? In true Mondays style, perhaps. There was a time, when they were skipping around Manchester selling this and that, that Happy Mondays began to attract the ever dubious tag of 'working class Tories'.Thatcher's true children. A joke? Shaun Ryder: "Well, maybe we fuckin' were. We listened to her. Of course we did. We fookin' listened to her every fookin' word and said, "Right bitch, we'll take you at your word." I've got to fucking cheer the bitch 'cos she got me off my arse."

Do you see there, smiling from beneath that quote, more than a small grudging respect? An ironic respect, maybe, but it was there all the same. One doubts that dear old Maggie would have quite approved of the manner in which Shaun accepted her advice. Take this little gem, from *Melody Maker*: "Thatcher turned straight people into criminals. If that's what we've got to call people who deal drugs, or whatever. I mean, we dealt, we did the lot. We sold fookin' Evian water that came straight out of the tap. They called us criminals, but the way we saw it, we were enterprising business people. She laid the cards out, man, and us people had no choice but to play her fookin' game. All that applies to us...and millions of fookin' others."

CHAPTER 15

"Manchester is not a nice place to be at the moment. It's too small and everybody is fucking up. Seventy five per cent of people in this city carry guns. They all think they're gangsters. There's so many fucking idiots in this place now, it's unreal."

Shaun Ryder

Oh, how the lad-mad-mag-men loved, and still love, Shaun Ryder. From the outset he was in there, an icon for the post-'right-on'-generation. The New Man antithesis, sneering and chortling bad boy, so ironically loved by women, loving to pose in and edit an edition of Penthouse. "I did it 'cos the money was fuckin good, innit." Oh, *Loaded*, this is your god!

Shaun on being irresistible to women: "I don't think I am, am I? I mean, me girlfriends have always been alright. I was always this mischievous, naughty lad, and a bit evil and ugly looking, and some chicks like that. In ten years I have had three serious relationships. In the first two relationships I did fuck about a lot and I've stepped out of line once or twice with Oriole (latter day girlfriend, daughter of Donovan, named after sixties soul label). But, because she grew up in the business, she can deal with it better. She's seen a lot of shit and she's a strong woman. I tell you, causal sex, right, it's always depended on if I'm off me nut. With skag, some people don't want to shag but, fucking hell, sometimes I'd be going for like fifteen hours. You don't come, man, with skag. It takes a hell of a long time to come when you are on gear and it was great when the chick didn't know you were stoned. After an hour she'd be going, "you haven't come, you haven't come" and I'd be thinking, fucking hell, don't hold your breath love, there's fourteen fucking hours to go yet."

Mad, mad Shaun, mocking the very notion of 'sexist', that horrendous grey word which throughout the seventies was duly bent this way and that, over-used as a weapon until it carried absolutely no meaning any longer. Until girls and boys alike would come out screaming, "Sod it all, we like shagging....okay?" Who better than Shaun to surf the backlash? He probably didn't know it, he certainly didn't plan it and the only book he had ever read, post-Suedehead, was Hunter Davies' Beatles tome.

Then a succession of events dissolved this likeable laddishness away, once and for all. It began, naturally, as a joke. A daft joke served to to alleviate the boredom of MTV. Shaun, sitting there, all smirky like a Grundy-ised Sex Pistol. Shaun joking on MTV. It was a *JOKE*. Shaun stated that he was...ahem, "a rent boy". Well, maybe it was just plain old naiveté, maybe it was some chemical talking or maybe he really was playing tricks with the media. How naive must Ryder have been? And could anyone be surprised when *The News Of The World* grasped this piece of mock information and plastered it across the nation's breakfast tables.

Shaun Ryder was not amused. He admitted, again and again, that he had dabbled in the peddling of drugs, thus causing him to become, in many people eyes, Public Enemy No. 1. The Sex Pistols may have sworn at a thoroughly deserving Bill Grundy, but all that, in retrospect, seemed astonishingly tame. Admitting to being a drug dealer at the point in history when drugs had started their terrifying seep into every British city was serious stuff. Yet it never worried Shaun a jot. However, being portrayed as a rent boy, even when he had instigated the story himself, caused him to fume. Was this his working class conservatism showing through?

Gunchester Rover

Shaun Ryder owned a gun. A 357 Magnum. French made. Nasty. Frightening, probably, not necessary. This coincided with Manchester's blackest spell to date, when the city's scene dipped into the gloom of so-called 'Gunchester'. Weapons became readily available in and around the areas of Moss Side and Cheetham Hill. Sensibly, the media's paranoia about firearms managed to soften a little, as the nineties wore on, and it was no longer considered cool to carry a fire arm. For a while, though, guns became the ultimate fashion accessory. Shaun Ryder owned a gun at a time when his mental state was highly unstable. Her never intended to use it but, there were forces circulating around the scene that were not altogether healthy. Shaun kept his gun quiet. It wouldn't, after all, be advisable to be seen actively promoting gun culture, to become a part of Gunchester. The problem with guns, however, is that they merely lie there, tempting the inevitable. Benign, silent, evil, they lurk in the drawer, under floorboards, clamped under cars, a tragedy waiting to happen, little time bombs of pain. Shaun's gun lay there, waiting. Soon enough came the inevitable. When *The News Of the World* ran the rent boy story depicting Ryder as some kind of low-slung male prostitute, most of the band, including Paul Ryder, merely laughed it off as little more than fizzy tabloid gush, which it was. Shaun however, never quite recovered from that. It put him in a darker, more unstable frame of mind. The article left him unbalanced. Unbalanced enough, he would admit, "To take my gun and blow a mirror in Dry Bar!"

It was Paul Ryder who broke the news to Shaun. He bounded into Shaun's bedroom, holding *The News Of The World* aloft. A fit of giggles. "Oh, maan, you've got problems, Shaun...You are in *The News Of The World* there, fucking rent boy...hahahah...fuckin' hell, X, what have you done?" Shaun leapt from the bed, grasped the paper and..."I nearly killed Paul. I said, "Fucking hell, ya fucking laffin', ya fuckin' laffin?" And I'd be chasing him around the house and he'd be laughing. Know what I mean?"

Andy Spinoza, co-founder of Manchester's *City Life* magazine, thought he knew. In 1991, he wrote "The Mondays were Thatcher's philosophy made sexy, made hip. At Dry Bar, staff wore T-shirts that read, 'Who put the Tory in Factory?"

This notion of Happy Mondays as working class Tory's was, also, a joke. But the fact was a that, since the *Bummed* sleeve, they had well and truly 'got up the noses of the more absurdly sanctimonious politicos.

All of this spilled over, in November 1991, in one of the *NME*'s most notorious and tabloid-esque features. Penned by Steven Wells - hardly Mr Right On, I seem to recall him, as a skinhead, sprawled over Gary Bushell's desk at *Sounds* in the late seventies - it proudly became a glorious catalyst for all manner of, in some cases, understandable hatred.

"So", asked Wells reasonably, "what's so bad about being called a rent boy?"

Ryder. "Lads who come from where I come from don't like being called a fucking faggot. I've got nothing against 'em, y'know what I mean, but I've got my rights and I ain't a fucking faggot and that's it. You know what I mean. Fuck it, I ain't going around bashin' 'em, I don't give a fuck. They can do what they want. But people, where I come from...that's probably the worst thing you could call somebody.."

"Being gay doesn't make you a rent boy."

"Right, alright, but I don't suck dick. Don't suck dick."

"The way you keep on using the words 'faggot' and 'pervert' has offended a lot of people."

"I don't give a fuck. I'm really not bothered. Before I came into this business, right, I came from north Manchester. I'd never met a homo before.....no, I hadn't. Ten years ago we was young boys and you come into this business and you meet gay people, right, and you think, "fuck". But then you think "No. Sound. Leave them alone." So I haven't got any problems and I ain't a fucking rent boy and it was a dirty story on me."

Later, Bez would famously join in the conversation: "I hate them (gays). To anyone whose a straight person, faggots are disgusting. Faggots might find shagging pussy disgusting, but we don't, we find...we find shagging a bloke not right. The majority of people in Britain aren't gay, are they?" And later, his streak of mild hypocrisy somewhat exposed as another member of the Mondays pointed out that Bez had recently spent time chatting amiably to Paul Rutherford and Boy George: "if he'd started getting his cock out in front of me, I'd have fucking killed the bastard."

The article continued in a similar vein, pushing the band further and further into this absurd foggy area of working class reactionaries, stubborn mock Tories, too thick to be flippant. Back at Factory, the article didn't, to say the least, go down incredibly well.

Tony Wilson. "We knew that Steven Wells came to Manchester to 'do' the Mondays. To set them up. It was all planned and we knew it. Perhaps the band brought it on themselves, but that's just the way they were, or are. Everyone knows that. They are the easiest band in the world to set up in such a way, simply because they are so honest. The *NME* knew that, as well...I mean they had had so much wonderful copy out of them. It was impossible to write a boring story about them, although, I must admit, Sarah Champion once managed it. But when that particular interview was over, we all sat back and waited for two weeks before it appeared in the paper. We thought it might be, you know, "Shock horror, the Mondays all drive BMW's, are they anti-socialist?". But we didn't realise it would be as bad as that....and that was it, really. Suddenly, as far as the music press were concerned, Happy Mondays were dead meat. No one wanted to know. The big story had blown and the writing was on the wall. I'm not bothered now, but I would have killed Wells at the time."

The interview was a death, of sorts. Of the Mondays, perhaps. After those few little words had so shocked the nations youth(!), things darkened considerably. Arguments flared within the band and within the crumbly old thing called Madchester. What chance now, The Mock Turtles, The Midwich Cuckoos, World Of Twist and all the breaking Manchester acts? And all of a sudden it wasn't such a great place to be anymore. Not that it had been eclipsed by any other music from any other town, and certainly not from the Thames Valley, but it was just wasn't the same. The Hacienda, after suffering the slings and arrows of police and thieves, of gangsters and officials, drugs and purists, had closed for a while, but was up and running again. There was even a fabulous, though fleeting, disco revival feel, revolving around one tumultuous night which even included an appearance by Sister Sledge. For a brief time, the street troubles at least superficially, seemed to have resided...but it felt wrong somehow. Gunchester, a flippant name for a very real danger, was brooding in the back alleys and pubs of Moss Side and Cheetham Hill, Rusholme and Ordsall, Openshaw and Stretford.

Despite considerable outside pressure following the *NME* article, Shaun refused to sack Bez who, according to Ryder, "had just got a bit wound up." The rest of the band, however, fully rounded on Bez, demanding he be dropped from the line up, accusing him of "fucking up" their careers, demanding, also, that his wages be stopped immediately. The ruptions were loud and vivid, the portents very bad indeed.

"We got turned over," admitted Shaun, "but that interview could have been written at any fucking point. That's how we always were. Yeah, so we shot our mouths off, most people do that, but most people don't have some cunt standing in front of them with a microphone. We should have known. We were stupid and skagged up. I was off me fuckin' head and so was Bez. Bez has a heart of gold, everyone knows that. But what really, really, pissed me off wasn't what was written at all, or the reaction of the twats who read and believe the *NME*...it was the rest of the band - the drummer, the bass player, the keyboardist - what a bunch of fucking hypocrites, man".

During one dreadful *Top Of The Pops* appearance, taking advice from friends who should have known better, Ryder not only sang live but also tried to sing 'straight'. Instead, he stumbled through, forgetting his lines. With the *NME* apparently turning away and turning readers away in droves, the vibe had been lost. Where was Bez on *Top Of The Pops*? Not sacked, but not there. It wasn't fun to be in the Mondays anymore. A letter arrived from the 'Aids Day' organisers, effectively banning Happy Mondays from the benefit. The letter quoted all of Bez's sorry words. Ryder knew the truth, the truth about Bez, but he couldn't use it. He knew that Bez had been banged up for robbery at the age of 17. He knew that Bez had single-handedly sorted out six sieg-heiling skinheads at a Leeds concert because he was worried they might cause offense. But it was no use. The rest of the band refused to enter the clubs of Manchester for weeks following the article. Their anger was directed partly at the *NME* and partly at Bez. Sometimes it's fun, sometimes it isn't. In truth, the band had all objected to Bez's words during the interview, but very little of that made it into print. They had wanted to say more, to say how they didn't dislike gays at all, but they were never allowed the chance. Suddenly, they were cast as outlaws. They had been banned from Dando's bar. Poor Rowetta, out on the town one night, found herself verbally abused, "Don't you bring your fucking mates in here," they screamed, "your Happy Mondays...homophobic bastards."

Manchester night life was floating heavily on the 'pink pound', in 1991. A self-confessed 'liberated city', at least according to the profoundly pro-gay town council, it made life extremely difficult for any night clubbing Mondays. Difficult and, in the face of a potential radical backlash, possibly very dangerous.

Nathan McGough had been furious as well. Furious with Shaun, as well as Bez who did, at least, have one excuse...he was Bez. McGough slammed Ryder for using the word "fag" and reminded him that Happy Mondays always had a small but enthusiastic gay audience. And what about the 'trannies' would adopt the song 'Mad Cyril' alongside their Judy Garland's and Liza Minnelli's. Now...all gone.

There were other internal problems too, that emerged with the 'Judge Fudge' *Top Of The Pops* appearance but, in truth, had been brooding away for some time - publishing money. It is a classic musical nightmare, and an all-too-easy route for band members disillusioned with their lot. The first few niggles came up in rehearsal, but eventually it was all-out war. Bad enough, one might reasonably assume, when the bass player requests decent royalties for the bass line he injected into the song written by the singer. That's a publishing classic (Andy

Rourke). Then there's the guitar - just how much of that guitar did Shaun think he owned? Who wrote that bit? And this bit? More difficult still, how did Bez come to be worth a royalty? The tit-fer-tat publishing rows had started to gnaw away at the inner workings of this band. It's true, Nathan should have spotted it. But if the Mondays had been anything like that then they wouldn't really have been the Mondays. Another slice of paradox.

Then came the big one. Bez, of course, had always been thick with Shaun, an unbreakable bond that would far outlive the band. But why should Bez get any royalties? The question was never successfully answered. Soon things worsened with band members haggling for the bigger profiles on TV appearances. Unbelievable that this should happen to the Happy Mondays.

Shaun Ryder: "A lot of what we said and what went down, around then, was simply to do with drugs. I can hardly remember any of it, anyway. There's a few little bits I can remember and bits of it are coming back, but mostly it's all a blur. The more I do remember the more embarrassed I get, so I generally try not to think about it. I don't think anything that I thought was really bad. We were just off our boxes, just daft lads. Didn't give a shit. Like, I called people a lot of names, caused a lot of problems, really, but it was just daft lads stuff. You see, we didn't give a fuck and, eventually, we got stitched up for it."

Fair enough? They'd had a damn good run, hadn't they? Got away with everything bar murder during their time. Were these the death throes of a great band? No. Worse, much worse was waiting, not just around the corner, but in the Caribbean.

CHAPTER 16

"I always said the better we got, there's no way we'd be wasting our money on drugs.We only took drugs in the first place because of boredom. Even if you have a gram-a-day heroin habit, it's cheaper than going water-skiing or windsurfing."

Shaun Ryder

One of the most glaring errors in the history of rock band management/label administration was to send Happy Mondays - a sinking ship, with all manner of music journalists leaping for the safety of the life rafts - to Barbados to record their follow up to *Pills, Thrills And Bellyaches*. Ironically, the financial stability of Happy Mondays wasn't anything like as healthy as one might have expected. That, of course, is one of the classic problems of any rollercoaster hedonistic rock act - money simply drips through their fingers, and everyone keeps smiling and saying nice things, and your life gets more and more frantic. Then suddenly people's attitude completely changes. They are pushing figures your way, demanding money back.. The party's over.

Nathan McGough was receiving phone calls, the kind of phone calls one receives when that old credit limit expires. Bizarre? Of course. This was a band whose last album had practically been a phenomenal success, surpassing all of Factory's expectations. Nevertheless, Nathan McGough knew full well that Happy Mondays were in desperate need of the advance that the recording of a new album would bring. He had no hesitation informing Tony Wilson that it would be hugely advantageous for the band to have an album recorded and released a soon as humanly possible. In truth, this was essential, not just for the band, but for the label as well.

By winter 1991, rumours around town were that Factory's finances were fucked, and that that they were likely to miss out on a buy-out by London Records if the situation was not rapidly and successfully addressed. Factory bosses knew that they needed product from their best-selling acts - New Order and Happy Mondays. Both bands professed to understand the situation and both bands knew, full well, that they had overspent, massively, during their last album recordings.Tony Wilson received assurances from managers McGough and Gretton that the new recordings would not cost more than £150,000. Inevitably, these predictions would prove woefully optimistic. The Happy Mondays album would cost £380,000 and New Order's a massive £430,000.

For Happy Mondays, who were, literally, sitting around Salford, waiting for McGough to wander in with a big new cheque, a shock was in store. Fiscal ineptitude, aesthetic misguidance (looking to record a Mondays album for £150,000, they nevertheless spent £200,000 on no-hope act Cath Carroll), and poor property investments had left Factory worth virtually nothing. For whatever reasons, the Mondays had to deliver. But artists, no matter who they are, cannot be expected to switch on and off in such a manner. Especially artists such as Shaun Ryder, unpredictable and capable of avalanches of creativity followed by deserts of blankness. Especially as the atmosphere within the Mondays camp had, for the first time since their initial stirrings, lost its shine. They were still mates but even that wasn't such a good thing. It prevented things from being said, it warped the dynamics of the band, it sat like a pressure cooker lid on a whole, seething mess of ego clashes. With the Mondays, with their apparently eternal looseness and, indeed, with their wild and hedonistic manager, things had been allowed to drift in a personal way. It was the true paradox of Happy Mondays, that the state of party cannot be eternal. That a band who survive for so long because of such camaraderie, eventually failed because of it.

Nevertheless, Shaun Ryder did, indeed, manage to find that burst of song writing creativity. McGough, inspired by his artists' unlikely positive reaction, informed Wilson that there was no reason why the band wouldn't be able to record an album in March, 1992. Both band and label agreed that a further collaboration with producers Oakenfold and Osborne would be highly desirable - every member of the band still adored Steve Osborne's knack of catching the pulse of the moment. Unfortunately, the producers were fully booked until June 1992 and, with fiscal pressure mounting dangerously, McGough and Wilson decided that the Mondays simply couldn't wait until then. Alas, this decision marked a souring of the relationship between Factory and Oakenfold and Osborne, who believed, and stated in print, that they had been tragically overlooked. This wasn't the case at all. The decision to approach ex-Talking Heads Chris Frantz and Tina Weymouth as alternative producers was instigated by sheer, financial necessity. The album *had* to be in the shops before the end of the year, even if it meant sending the band to the other end of the world to do it.

Dangers In Paradise, Barbados, March 1992

Tina Weymouth: "Coming from the New York scene we have met, and worked with, all kinds of freaks and weirdos. But they always, when it came down to it, they always turned out to be pretty normal people underneath. It was the old rock thing...a show. People, I thought, are all basically the same. But when we met and worked with the Mondays, I finally realised that, well, they were different. They were for real. They lived it, everyday. I never knew that people like that existed."

Initially, Happy Mondays had wished to record the *Yes Please* album at the legendary Compass Point Studios in Nassau, Bahamas and it was there that a small Mondays delegation met and immediately bonded with Chris and Tina. The studio, although enwrapped in scenic splendour, had seen better days and seemed to lag a long way behind the state-of-the-art ideal. This was naturally a huge disappointment, tempered only by the belief that Chris and Tina might just be an inspired choice. They were hardly aloof, techno-headed producers, these were *band* people. They understood the dynamics of a band, even a band like Happy Mondays. Enlivened by the prospect of working with such producers, Happy Mondays regained that all essential vibe, that frisson, even that camaraderie. This was encouraging and, fuelled further by tales of Shaun Ryder's sudden bursts of songwriting - things looked curiously, perhaps disturbingly, optimistic. The band had a meeting and decided that, this time, they would not fall apart in a mess of drugs and alcohol, they would be content to knuckle down. The band determined not just to be a bunch of drug crazed lunatics, high on luck and nerve, they now expressed a desire to become known as serious artists, as a genuine working unit. This was the vibe which flew back and forth along the telephone lines between Tina and Chris and the band, prior to the recording. Ironically it was this new-found work ethic and camaraderie in one half of the band that presaged their split, for it was not shared by Shaun and Bez. From hereon, the Mondays were destined to implode.

The new location would be Eddie Grant's studio, Blue Wave. True to the mighty legacy of the great reggae studios, it was fantastically equipped and yet housed in what amounted to little more than a shanty shack, slap bang in the centre of a sugar plantation, miles from anywhere or anything. The band claimed that Barbados was chosen for recording because of the studio location. Wilson and Factory claimed it was because of the island's reputation for being heroin-free, a place where Ryder could chill out, get out of the addiction and get down to business. "What a fucking laugh that was," states Wilson, "True, there was no heroin on the island but what we didn't know was that it was a fuckin' crack island! The worst place on earth to send Shaun."

It was worse than Tony Wilson and Nathan McGough could envisage. Shaun Ryder was in a deep heroin habit. So deep, in fact, that his every waking move bore the legendary cunning of a junkie. He knew full well that the reason for sending the band to Barbados had little to do with Factory wanting the lads to record in a wonderful, relaxing place. He knew the rumours, that it was a non-smack island but even if that were untrue, this place was well outside his network of dealers. No matter. Shaun Ryder put his emergency plans into action. For a start, he turned up at Heathrow's departure lounge armed with 3,000 milligrams of quality methadone. The junkie's legal equivalent to smack, methadone is intended to lure the addict slowly out of the depths of addiction but is used, more often than not, as a straight substitute. Ryder's plans crashed disastrously when he dropped the methadone container in the airport. Pools of quality meth, spilling out of the container, growing into a methadone lake, right there in Heathrow Airport. Ryder's accompanying 'minders' began scurrying to and fro, scooping the liquid up into any makeshift container they could find, at times, scooping up chunks of broken glass as well. Not that Ryder minded. Only able to see to his next hit, he resigned himself to a diet of crunchy methadone. They managed to rescue 120 milligrams, all of which he drank the moment he stepped onto Barbados soil. Illustrating the intensity of Ryder's addiction was his daily dose - 120 milligrams - a serious amount. A potentially deadly addiction. Once on the island, making a mockery of the idea that he would clean up, Ryder immediately changed from smack to crack, one of the most notoriously dangerous changes of diet in junkie culture.

Tina and Chris soon had the band settled and working, but as soon as Ryder arrived, the problems started to pile up. He was in no fit state to write or record, unlike the rest of the sober band. As Derek Ryder pointed out, when the leader lets the band down, it isn't long before the whole thing starts to crumble. The rifts between Shaun, Bez and the rest of the band cracked wide open and left the producers stunned, as one thing after another went wrong in slapstick yet tragic fashion.

Barbados was clearly not the ideal place to let the Mondays settle for various reasons. The searing, relentless, mind-warping sunshine. Pouring down like gold on the lush, dark, greenery. Brought up on stolen cars driven at break-neck speed around England's north west, Bez was unprepared for the snaking, pot-holed local roads cut into gaping gorges. Broken roads, patrolled by wild dogs, loose cattle and spliff-heavy pedestrians, incapable of walking in a straight line, the highways would be treacherous enough for decent vehicles. The dubious hire vehicles with dodgy brakes and dirt-laden interiors that Bez found himself throwing around the dusty mountain roads were a far cry from Salford. It wasn't long before his arm was broken, as he crashed his Jeep while doing a cool 55mph down a dirt track built for the speeds of a heavily laden ox. Given the availability of the most body-draining weed, gallons of rum and the fiercest crack, it was no surprise when a boating accident caused him to break it again. For luck, the third assault on Bez's arm was completed by his girlfriend sitting on it. Several months were spent with the arm strapped in a most peculiar Heath Robinson affair. The kind of thing which Bez, and only Bez, could turn into a fashion item - which he duly did. Looking back at such an unstable cocktail, all anyone could do was stand back and wait for it to happen.

Meanwhile, crack and Shaun was proving to be an unhealthy mix. While the band waited by their instruments in the studio, Shaun was locked in the toilet for 20 hours a day, smoking rocks, a lost cause. Back in Manchester and more so in the grubbier corners of a couple of tabloids, it was being reported that Shaun Ryder had completely lost his mind, while the rest of the band were running around in a drug-crazed wife-swapping orgy. Ryder was reported to be doing 600 grams of crack a day. He would later refute this. For what it's worth, his daily intake was about twenty rocks of coke a day. As each rock contained 20 grams, the drug rumours, at least, weren't that wide of the mark.

Tony Wilson: "I heard reports, I kept getting bizarre messages. Fact is, Factory was teetering on the brink and our only chance to escape seemed to lie in the hands of this crazy bunch of useless fucks who were speeding around Barbados, crashing into fucking trees. Within the first seven days there were three major car smashes. I was in L.A. at that point and I was only there for four days before I had to get back to do some filming for Granada. So I thought I might fly down to

Barbados and see what was happening. That was my idea, to call in on the way home. But I couldn't believe where Barbados was somewhere off the coast of Venezuela. It seemed too far to travel, so I simply decided not to go. Probably that was the most expensive mistake of my life because, well, maybe, just maybe, I might have been able to do something. I've regretted it ever since." It is doubtful whether the arrival of Wilson would or could have made the slightest difference. What he would have encountered would have been two stunned producers, sitting alone in an apparently trashed studio, shaking their heads in disbelief."

Tina and Chris, in true American tradition, and with genuine enthusiasm and regard for the band and their music, tried so desperately to keep the ship afloat. However, by the time it got to the stage of "how many members of the band are in hospital this morning?", even this professional devotion began to wane. Nevertheless, they were troupers and, despite the fact that the band were all running round, arguing, smashing cars and smoking rocks while they really should have been finishing the guide vocals, they somehow managed to maintain their sense of perspective. The rest of the band - who seriously longed to concentrate on the work - were seriously pissed off with Shaun's flippancy, with his total inability to concentrate and his apparent lack of any urgency. Whether he was fully aware of Factory's genuinely precarious fiscal position or not remains unclear. Later he would famously state: "I don't give a fuck about *Yes Please*. It were shite. We did it to help Factory out. That, and we could record it in the Bahamas, (though, actually, it was Barbados), which meant we'd get the royalties Factory owed us in the form of a holiday." But the truth of the matter was that, when Factory collapsed, Happy Mondays would be owing the label £430,000, rather than vice versa. They would have little to complain about. He would also refer to it as "a fucking fantastic time...a great, month-long holiday in which, yes, alright, there were a few mad bits, but I really enjoyed myself over there...and so did the rest of the band."

It wasn't, of course, a fantastic time at all. In all fairness to

Shaun, he had spent two years in a constant state of touring and promoting and, despite the previously alleged burst of artistic energy, arrived on the island in a state of severe exhaustion, with no real new material on paper. To make matters worse, due to a drug related throat infection (this was due to the crack which plays havoc with the tonsils), there was absolutely no chance of laying down any vocals. No wonder he freaked out. Worse than this, he believed that his frantic lifestyle had blotted out his moments of reflection, of contemplation. He had simply lived the life without, as he would put it, "having any time to take things in....those two years had been a total blur." "Shaun," Tina stated, "you have all these demons inside you and that is why you get stoned like this..there is something eating you up inside. Let's find out what it is then deal with it, shall we?"

It was, in truth, a genuinely caring attitude but one which was rather wasted on Ryder. He had no choice but to leave the island, with the album barely started, and opt for a course in a Chelsea de-tox centre.

CHAPTER 17

May 1992, Recording at Comfort Place Studios, Surrey

After Barbados, the band re-grouped with their producers at Comfort Place Studios. Things appeared to have improved. Shaun was happy for a while, scribbling lyrics down in frantic, almost panicky manner, trying to capture the moment, digging into his memory and pulling out all manner of surreal bits and bobs and hazy dreams. For a while Shaun thought it might work, too. Nathan worried that he had started to push his artist too hard - he had. Over-aware of the need for caution after the *NME* interview - it wouldn't do to offend further - Ryder found it hard to work within unwritten but understood boundaries. He had to be "double, double careful." There was no fun in song writing if he couldn't push it all the way. But this time he just couldn't. And he knew that his band wouldn't sound like a band having fun. It would be forced. Chris and Tina knew this. They knew the signs. As two of the most intelligent popsters of the past two decades, Chris and Tina knew, full well, that this band was exploding or imploding...losing it either way. They concentrated on diversionary tactics. On attempting to summon a muse for Shaun, they tried a few weird things, like an out-take from *Spinal Tap*. Getting Shaun to throw coins and consult the I Ching (can you imagine?) which he obediently did. They even made him do a few daft dances, just to lift the spirits. Like the Peppermint Twist! Shaun laughed and messed about. He thought he was helping Chris. Chris thought he was helping Shaun. Nathan looked on, helplessly. The wheels had come off. You could see it in Nathan's face. He knew it. Shaun probably knew it too but he was willing to go along with the ride. If the aesthetic vision of Happy Mondays, the hip street suss and verve, was to crash headlong into a brick wall...then, fuck it. It had been a good ride. On with the next thing. That was

Shaun...he *knew* it had gone. Fuck Factory. Fuck Chris and Tina. Fuck responsibility, friends and career. Ryder knew his moment had passed with the Mondays. If Factory's future depended on his coming up with the goods, then it was clearly not going to happen. The muse would not return...not with this band. Chris and Tina were going to be hard-pushed to make an album out of this material, and with such an atmosphere developing in the band it was highly unlikely. There was pure hatred.

Ryder later told *Melody Maker*: "It all got so fucking obnoxious, it had turned into the total fucking opposite of what we'd started out doing in the first place. You know, in the early days we all had input. I could say, "try this, do that, whatever." And we'd try loads of different stuff. That's what made the Mondays what they were. But by the time we came to record that last thing, we were all off on our own little trips. Even when we were playing live we weren't playing as a band, we was playing as fucking individuals. Everybody hated each other so bad in the end. It was impossible to talk. It was like, "I play the fucking drums, so fuck off, I play the keyboards, so fuck off, I play the guitar, so fuck off.""

Shaun Ryder was fat, thin, fat, thin, bloated, haggered, depending on which paper you picked up, and in which week. Permanently binging on drugs and booze, it had to stop, he knew it. He'd been in re-hab a couple of times in the Priory Clinix Rehabilitation in Hale, Cheshire. He'd also had a spell down at Charter Clinic in London, where the patients are edged into a twelve point recovery plan. One of the key aspects of that course was a belief in God. Luckily for Ryder, it was explained that God could be substituted by someone, a Granny perhaps, who they respected and admired. This time, determined to work through the entire course, Ryder knew he would have to accept a little 'brainwashing'. Previous re-hab visits had all failed because he had left the course before the psychotherapy had started. He had a natural aversion of people taking control over him and, even at Charter Clinic, he would initially find himself fighting it. The experience would surface in the song title 'Stinkin' Thinkin'', which collated all the thoughts one washes away while going through therapy to get straight. Later Ryder would, sadly, reflect that, if something good came out of the re-hab experience, then it was that song. There were the sessions which Ryder rather perversely enjoyed, and which reminded him of those old drama classes back at school. He would sit as part of a wide, half circle, and be forced into confession: "Hi, I'm Shaun and I'm a recovering junkie." This, at least, he found illuminating. He glanced around the class and knew in his heart that he didn't want to be a junkie anymore.

For a while, it was great being straight. A month away from drink and drugs. Drifting around Cornwall. Attending a Northern Soul evening and feeling fourteen again. Allowing the beat to sink firmly in, affecting his thoughts, like an old Motown disco, a soundtrack to a teenage romance. For a while, if only in that club, the magic returned to Shaun Ryder. The crowd was refreshingly old. Old Northern Soul fanatics simply having a great time, spinning, dipping and shuffling, with not a care in the world, where hipness mattered not. No-one bothered if the correct pair of trainers were worn and no-one mocked the DJ for playing the odd corny tune. It was northern soul...just like in the old days. Alcohol free revelry, whoops, howls and air punching, great, affecting music and great, timeless dancing, beer bellies and sagging bottoms. Shaun Ryder chilled out. Lovely to be among people who just wanted to be there. How different to the hardcore club he would visit, just days later, which, in Shaun's words, was simply "hateful." All poise, noise and no melody. Shaun Ryder was growing old.

Yes Please

Tony Wilson: "Everyone hated *Yes Please*, everyone slagged it, including the band but, in the end, how bad was that album? I remember getting the tape and playing it over and over again in the office. And I thought the songs were great. I thought the production was even great...that was a great fucking album, man. For a while, I couldn't understand why Shaun hated it so much, why Bez slagged it off, why all the band refused to even acknowledge it as a proper Mondays album. Maybe they were starting to believe their own bad press. It happens."

To outside ears, ie. anyone not in someway connected with Happy Mondays, *Yes Please* might sound like a fine, if flawed, record. True enough, it fails to swell with the fresh swagger of *Pills, Thrills and Bellyaches*. It could, indeed, be that difficult third album that came one record late. But to all involved, *Yes Please* is little more than a bundle of pain, of broken friendships, broken dreams and sheer, dogged hard work conducted for the sake of contractual obligation. If Happy Mondays had originally been a perfectly natural state of party, then this was the recording of the morning after.

The squabbles in the band ballooned into all manner of conflicts. The aforementioned rifts had begun when certain factions within the band began taking things a little too seriously. Happy Mondays were never, ever, meant to be serious. The writing had been on the wall for some time, ever since one band member turned up at a meeting with an idea to instigate personal pensions plans. Personal pensions? For Happy Mondays?

Nevertheless, for the press, these chasms were swiftly papered over. Shaun became all lovely, "well, we have been through hell but we are mates, really." For a while, it seemed easier for the band to believe that rather than face reality. After all, another dark cloud was looming. Factory Records were edging closer and closer towards receivership.

Despite the success of Happy Mondays and New Order, despite the cashing in on Madchester, despite enormous potential and remarkable successes, Factory blew it. The beginning of the end can be traced back to one of the very reasons for the label's success, to that fabulous 'up' period which followed on the heels of New Order's *Substance*. Factory, having purchased the aforementioned Charles Street building for £100,000, would eventually spend £750,000 on transforming it into a needlessly stylish office. The building had several strange luxuries - a zinc roof which no-one could see, as well as a suspended board room table that was subsequently destroyed during a bout of Happy Mondays horseplay. It was a wonderfully absurd Factory thing to do. This was a building that, unlike The Hacienda, unlike the company's Dry Bar on Oldham Street, couldn't earn its keep. It was purchased right at the peak of the property boom. Factory had also finally purchased the building which housed The Hacienda. This was a fiscal disaster that verged on sheer genius. Factory decided that, if they secured a mortgage in Germany, which they could on their German earnings, then they would be paying a far lower interest rate. Unfortunately, before being able to approach the German banks, they needed to secure a six month stop-gap mortgage.

Unfortunately, within those six months, two positively awesome changes in climate would take place. Firstly, the scene would twist horribly, from the hedonistic glories of Madchester to the dark stirrings of Gunchester. Indeed, it was to be the most tumultuous six months in Manchester night clubbing history, as the drug gangs of Moss Side and Cheetham Hill moved in on the city centre. Most notoriously they homed in on The Hacienda, capturing along the way a smattering of gloatingly savage international headlines. Simultaneously, Factory's split with Rough Trade in Europe, caused the German idea to collapse. What this meant was that Factory, following the dreadful publicity, wouldn't be able to capture a mortgage anywhere, in England or Germany, and were forced into paying the stop-gap rate, a whopping eight per cent over the base rate. Just at this point, as they were forced into paying 23% interest rate on The Hacienda, the property boom collapsed. In the space of three months, the value of The Hacienda plummeted from £1,000,000 to £300,000, leaving Factory swimming in negative equity. Needless to say, the £750,000 spent on the company's Charles Street headquarters now seemed even more absurd.

All this and an album, from their No. 1 artists, Happy

Mondays, which bombed out of sight. Yet still Factory were hoping that London Records would buy them out of their impossible situation. In a meeting with Polygram, Factory's back-catalogue looked like the detail that might make the purchase worthwhile. Then, someone in the Factory team remembered a little insignificant piece of paper, dated 1979, which stated, "The musicians own the music and we own nothing. Signed: A. Wilson, A. Erasmus, R. Gretton."

Originally intended to secure and maintain Factory's naive 'indie' dream, this little semi-contract effectively wiped off the value of all company's assets. London had little choice but to retreat, to wait for Factory to crumble to dust, and then begin foraging among the rubble. London were guilty of nothing. Indeed, eventually, when the label finally collapsed, they would create a new Factory, Factory Too which effectively left Happy Mondays free to negotiate with anyone they wished.

But the band had gone anyway. Their British tour, hastily arranged to promote *Yes Please*, was as sad as an ex-punk band on a tour of working men's clubs. Harry (Gio Goi employee, Mondays devotee): "I recall sitting in the Mondays dressing room, where was it? Newcastle, I think, and it was weird. Stony silence. That whole state of party had completely gone and you just knew that this was a band, who had once had the ball, had lost it. It wasn't all their fault...not just that stupid *NME* interview. I mean, the Mondays had got too tied up with that Madchester thing so when it started to fade there was absolutely nothing you could do about it. It was odd because it looked as if The Stone Roses were going to go on and become, I don't know, bigger than Led Zep or something. You just expected them to go on and on and on...and here was the Mondays. Getting smaller and smaller. I'd seen it before, with many, many bands. Even your inspiration goes out the window. There's fuck all anyone could do. Well, that was what it was like in that dressing room and it was massively embarrassing, because you just didn't know what to say. I mean, Shaun would come over and you just wanted to chat to him and say, "Hey, Shaun, don't worry, it will be alright, that was a great show tonight." The only thing was that it *wasn't* a great show at all. It had been crap. If you take the spirit away from the Mondays, then you take everything away, don't you. Shaun knew it was crap, so you were placed in an impossible position. Whatever you said would either sound like bullshit or very patronising...or you could tell him the truth. But how can you say, "Hey Shaun, you were really shit tonight and it looks like the Mondays are all washed up."? It was horrible."

Although Factory's problems were not solely pinned on the Mondays, the negative vibes from that camp certainly helped to intensify the feeling that something was lost. On their final US tour, the Factory office had been inundated with faxes from disgruntled promoters, from disgruntled fans even. The chief complaint was that Happy Mondays (never, as previously explained, being ones to overstay their welcome on stage), had trimmed their set from a barely tolerable (by US standards) fifty minutes to a clearly absurd twenty minutes. "Shaun," screamed Wilson during one heady confrontation, "you are doing twenty minute sets, for fucks sake." "Twenty five minutes," replied an indignant Ryder. "Yes Shaun, but that includes the encore, doesn't it." At one notorious US gig, watched by a Quentin Tarantino entourage, who were apparently inspired by the sheer gall of the band, they exited the stage after just five tuneless minutes and, legend still has it, were "extremely brassed off" when the venue owner refused them payment.

Back in 1991, Shaun Ryder had made, as Lou Reed once said, a very big decision. He had reached the end. The decision was simple - either come off the smack or die. He chose the former by opting, as is the way, for methadone. At first the doses were huge and he would frequently top the methadone up with heroin. Eventually, over nine months later, he had managed to bring the daily dosage down to a manageable amount. Unfortunately, by this time the drop in the levels had started to affect him in other ways. "It was getting me in the mind...that's what I couldn't handle," he told *Melody Maker*. So Ryder switched to valium and, eventually Prozac. And it was Prozac that effectively saved Shaun Ryder. Until that point, his addiction hadn't really been cured, it had been merely stifled. Prozac was the true cooler. It provided him with the immense strength needed to defeat a serious nine year habit.

Of course, he had no choice, really. The whole point of Happy Mondays was that they did exactly what they wanted, all the time. Do music, do drugs, sell drugs, have a laugh. Fall in line with their urges - but that creates a problem. What begins as a strength soon becomes a weakness. By the time Shaun Ryder was 33 years old, he found himself wandering around Manchester and Salford, looking at 'old' blokes, covered in spots, drained by alcohol or drugs. Two things dawned on him. One would be that he vowed never to end up like that and the other was that many of these guys, dashing from pub to pub, weren't really old at all. They were the same age as him. The signs were there alright. The demons were wandering around Manchester.

Bez, strangely, had never been into smack. He was a dope, speed and ecstacy man. Perhaps *the* dope, speed and ecstacy man of all time, but, to this day he will adamantly state that he isn't, and never was, neither an alcoholic nor a drug addict. How frightening to think, the *Melody Maker* once opined, that the most sensible member of Happy Mondays would be Bez - amazingly, he was the only member of the band to take old Maggie Thatcher's advice and secure a mortgage during the bands existence.

Manchester Evening News, Wednesday, 25th November, 1992

"Mondays Up For Grabs: Happy Mondays are ready to negotiate a new deal within hours of the collapse of their record company, Factory. Happy Mondays revealed the collapse would rid them of all contractual obligations. "We are looking forward to a new start," stated manager Nathan McGough. "We will negotiate a worldwide deal. It is not the end of an era, it's just business and, in this climate, everyone has to be ready for things like this."

Nathan McGough scoffed at claims that delays in the completing of the new Happy Mondays album could be blamed for Factory's collapse: "I think it made very little difference, if any, to the collapse. I know how much money is outstanding and even if the record had sold three million copies, it would have made very little difference." The band state: "It is with regret that we received the news with regard to Factory being placed in receivership. We are sorry for those who have lost their jobs, some of whom have given great support to Happy Mondays. We realise this will cause hardship for the creditors, some of whom worked very closely with us and we regard as friends. For those who are concerned, we wish to make it clear that the closure will cause very few problems for Happy Mondays. It will free the band. We hope that Factory could be sold as a going concern and we would be happy to discuss the possibility of working with Factory again should that be the case."

They wouldn't, of course, work with Factory again. They wouldn't work with anyone again. Not together. Not as a team, as a gang, as a band, as a drunk-on-funk whole, not as anything. The truth is that, with or without the Factory collapse, Happy Mondays had effectively split up during (if not before) the recording of *Yes Please*. They knew it. They knew it back then, when Shaun Ryder's drug habit had overcome his sense of balance, when his state of mind, blowing hot and cold no longer carried any responsibility towards Happy Mondays. The band were cast into the undertow and the friendships, long since withered, had finally, miserably, completely snapped. Gone. Did the band really expect to carry on? Did they really think that Nathan McGough's frantic efforts to secure a decent new major label recording contract would be enough to magically fuse the Mondays back together? There is no doubt about it, such a situation would have been the most terrible sham. You cannot invent or re-invent a band like Happy Mondays. They just have to happen.

Nevertheless, there was hope. For a while, there was a large, hugely optimistic deal with EMI sitting on the table, literally awaiting signatures. Nathan had worked hard. EMI Director Clive Black sat with the smiling band, waiting to complete the deal. Shaking with paranoia, confused by circumstances and narcotics, Ryder simply stood up and waltzed out of the room, leaving the remaining Happy Mondays staring into blankness. All those years of work had combined to get them into that room with someone as important as Clive Black, and with EMI happy to come up with the goods - and in two minutes, all that optimism, all those futures, just disintegrated into nothing.

Ryder later called a band meeting with a view to patching things back up but even he could do nothing to salvage the situation. Ryder duly apologised, but it would be too difficult to rekindle the EMI interest, and besides, the band had finally run out of patience. It was over. Happy Mondays were dead and buried.

CHAPTER 18

"I'm not an alcoholic. I was a drug addict. My liver's a bit hard, but all the damage that's been done to me's really by doing drugs, and that can be repaired. If you're an alcoholic, you're finished."

Shaun Ryder

The post-Mondays, pre-Black Grape Shaun Ryder was not a pretty sight. Not that he has ever been a picture, but his appearance did seem to take a turn for the worse. Monday's close follower, Harry, a Wythenshaw ex-pirate merchandiser, Gio Goi salesman and latter-day tour manager, recalls seeing Ryder slouched grumpily behind the wheel of his BMW, driving around the winding, leafy lanes of Cheshire looking for some kind of escape, a breath of freedom, a way out. Cheshire is often regarded as a plush out-post, a rural wilderness for Salfordians who have made some money. It is also the perfect county for local drug dealers to find refuge - and they are there, right now, the ex-hard men, sipping real ale and eating rare steaks, in Wilmslow, Prestbury and Alderley Edge. Harry recalls: "I'd only seen him, well, it seemed like a few weeks before. I'd spent some time on that last Mondays tour and, as I've said, it was the saddest thing I'd ever seen. They were my favourite band, they were us. And then weeks later, seeing Shaun near where I live and hardly recognising him, man. He had put on an awful lot of weight. He looked haggered, defeated. It was pretty sad. I mean, I don't know where his head was at, but it certainly looked as though he needed time out."

Of the period, where a moustache even mysteriously appeared, Ryder would later say: "Well, yeah, but it wasn't as sad as all that. People were telling me that I was washed up, that I had blown it with the Mondays and that I would never do anything again. But I knew it was not like that at all. In a sense, I felt free, it felt refreshing to have lost all those shackles.

I had also stopped doing gear, man. It was the first time in years that I hadn't needed to be stoned in order to get through the day. To get my work done. I was double straight. When the Mondays had finished, everyone legged it and there was an awful lot of shit to be cleared up and I was the one who had to do that. I was responsible...frozen assets an' all that...fucking hell, man. But the funny thing was that I started to really enjoy myself. I was having the best time, and it was great to see all these people say that I was washed up. I remember that driving round Cheshire bit...fuckin laugh that was."

September 1993 Treading Water

In 1993, as a dreary spring twisted into a dreary summer, the post-Monday's dust began to settle and all the concerned parties seemed to vanish into a relatively silent Manchester scene. Manchester was transient, rather than finished, and despite the city being thoroughly written off as 'old hat' by the inky music weeklies, the signs were in place for yet more to happen. After all, within a couple of years, the city would be boasting the biggest rock band in the world, the biggest pop act in the world and the biggest adult pop act in the world.

Having said that, by 1993, to have been connected, however tentatively, to the old Madchester explosion, was to find yourself firmly sliding down the wrong side of the fame pyramid. The small acts vanished by the dozen. Even the big acts had lost the impetus. The Stone Roses *Second Coming* might have changed things, but it was too difficult to mask half a decade of arsing around in Welsh cottages. Inspiral Carpets were still in swing but, even there, the writing was on the wall - at the first possible opportunity, they were tragically and unfathomably dropped by their label, Mute. Against this tide, there were some signs that a few record industry moguls were still nurturing a faith in the city. Pete Waterman attempting, as he still is, to spin his image around from King Of Crap to Doyen Of Dance, had purchased a lovely but derelict church at the hip Knott Mill end of Deansgate, around the corner from The Boardwalk and The Hacienda. Employing a heady mixture of bright young post-grads and wayward hedonists, he had started to build an impressive, subterranean studio complex, the first part of which had been in place before the Mondays split. One recalls the pre-split band booking in with intent to record a fifth album in there, the choice of venue being "the opposite of fucking Barbados, like." After one meeting with a clearly shaken Nathan McGough, however, studio manager Paul Waterman was heard to unwittingly express the somewhat hilarious words "Was he on drugs, or what?"

After the fall, however, various ex-Mondays would flit in and out of the complex, which also included young industry promotions company, Red Alert. Pretty soon, hot gossip within those dusty corridors spread rumours of a new band, a cocktail of ex-Smiths and ex-Mondays. They would eventually surface, and then vanish, as Delicious.

After that stifled glimpse of hope...silence. Bez, whose Barbados exploits had fully cemented his enviable reputation as 'head nutter', would occasionally drift into town. Like a cartoon character having fallen into the Grand Canyon, his broken arm was held aloft in a bizarre space age contraption which made several proud appearances in Manchester clubs. It even helped to gain him more than a few column inches in the *Manchester Evening News* pages. Bez had finally become a bona fide local celebrity - encircled by the true new pops stars of the city, the young breed of footballers...Sharpe, Giggs, Nicky Summerbee. Then he'd appear in Home nightclub, in The Boardwalk, smiling for the local paparazzi. Falling in line alongside Caroline Aherne, Hooky, Clint Boon, Mick Hucknall, Kevin Kennedy, Terry Christian and a whole string of would-be's and could-be's. How odd.

Although Derek Ryder was becoming more and more active on the local band scene, mixing here and there, producing demos, associating himself with genuine enthusiasm, to no small number of 'would-be's, Shaun generally kept himself out of harm's way. There was an infamous and clumsy appearance on *The Word*, just at the point when everything was falling around him, during which he referred to Gary Whelan as, most tellingly, "that drummer bloke." Surely, there would be no way back from that?

His personal life popped and splattered into the gossip columns, which must have been at once pleasing and yet irritating. People were still interested although many others, including dozens of Madchester bands who hadn't made it, now relished the prospect of seeing Ryder fall to earth. He had the ball once, they said, and now he's lost it and just doesn't have the talent to pick it up again. That was the vibe in Manchester, not among his legion of Salfordian mates, but for the envious masses, for whom there is no sweeter sight than a fallen star. What would Ryder do? What could Ryder do? One had to admit, the odds didn't seem exactly encouraging. At home, Ryder had left his long term girlfriend, Trisha McNamara and had started to date Oriole Leitch, daughter of Donovan, a very public liaison. The ruptions in Manchester continued to be noisy and vicious: "He's had a nervous breakdown," one gossipy voice claimed, in a fit of glee. Many doubted that we would hear Shaun's gruff, lovably tuneless, strangely charismatic, oddly warming voice again.

*   *   *

Ryder was, however, soon back on one of the tracks on the new EP by one of the genuine survivors of Madchester, Interstella. The band were a lightly funky and likeable post-Madchester crew fronted by the stunning Stella - ex-girlfriend of Nathan McGough, a woman of steely determination, blessed with a deliciously sensuous voice. Although the single's A side was 'The Drifter', it was 'Can You Fly Like You Mean It Gun-gadin?' that grasped the attention. A strange song, in which Stella's lilting voice was countered by Ryder's harsh growl. *Melody Maker* immediately picked up on the unlikely liaison and dispatched writer Paul Lester to grab the story, splashing

Shaun and Stella across the front page, looking like a couple who had just turned up at a building society, hoping to secure a mortgage for their starter home. Perhaps true to this image, the liaison would, alas, end in unholy conflict.

Nevertheless, at least Shaun looked well, his badly besuited appearance making him look like a trainee salesman at a particularly parochial branch of Dixons. He proved to be both awkward and gloriously quotable for the *Melody Maker* journalist. Not at all like the man I'd met, just days earlier, in The Canal Bar, who told me "I never really gave a fuck about anything so why should I start now...I'm happy being me and I might not, I just might not make any records anymore. I'm, sick and tired of celebrity, it's all bullshit, anyway." That day he had been swigging lager and laughing and appeared relieved not to be carrying the weight of a band, or a career on his shoulders. He would suggest to Paul Lester that "I'm not in the music business anymore, this is just a one off," but the Shaun Ryder I met didn't seem to square with the Shaun Ryder who appeared in *Melody Maker*...apparently wishing to settle the odd score. He attacked record company personnel and even the bods from Factory records, with lines like these: "Obviously people weren't even listening to the music. It just seemed like loads of people were signing up bands and then, ten minutes later, deciding to drop them. They didn't even listen to the fucking bands. They just wanted to make a lot of money. It was just like the Stock exchange...buy Manchester, buy, buy...okay...sell Manchester, sell, sell." And then out spilled the bitterness. There was a certain amount of tension in the air at this meeting, and Ryder didn't retreat when it was suggested that the music press had actually helped Happy Mondays. Indeed, one might add, without the *NME* and *Melody Maker*, would he not be still languishing on the dole?
"Yeah....until a lot of snotty little kids start writing for certain papers. I just think some of the kids who write for such magazines should have a smack on the head and be told that they can't write on their own without stabilisers until they are 22. 'Til they start appreciating music, whether it's Frank

Sinatra or Interstella. It's all music, it's music. And then you get some snotty kid writing in some magazine sayin' this is great and he's into it now, and in one year's time he's slagging off what he was into. There's not enough people liking music for what it is...I don't need my dick sucked by the media or anyone else. I don't need to get involved with the music business, the press or anybody in England. I haven't done anything recently, but I believe in this band and their music."

There was a defensive edge to Shaun, a natural state of post-band aggression. However, there was a little more than that. Happy Mondays had, after all, been more than a band. Several deep friendships were lost in the mess at the end. Shaun: "For a few years, we had good fun and me and Mark Berry made the music business interesting, turning it into a black comedy. But people didn't want fucking fun so it's no skin off my nose...it just used to get on my tits when there would be three million people who would buy *The Sun* and they'd be sayin' to us "Why did the Mondays split?" or whatever when a few thousand people had been shot to death (in Yugoslavia). I mean, as if a fucking band splitting up is important. It all seemed fucking stupid to me. Our time had ended, you know. It ended for the people in the band and that's it. I mean, what do you say? You turn into your father. Well, apart from me and Bez, the rest of the band turned into Mark Day's father. It was old and finished."

There, in a sense, was the real clue. Shaun and Bez sticking together through it all. No one quite knew how Bez might spend the rest of his life, least of all Bez himself, but, if nothing else, the strand of friendship with Shaun had not been severed. After all that had happened they were, it now seemed, like any other band, rubbed away with clashing ego's and differences prized open by money.

Shaun: "Obviously certain people started thinking about money, money, money all the time and once you start thinking like that..." Cracks opened and Happy Mondays fell into several strands. Paul Davis and Gary Whelan did, at least, stick together with a gleeful Davis stating at the time, "I feel terrific about the split. It's the best thing I've ever done. I'm just sorry it didn't happen sooner." The truth was that Davis and Whelan had been working on and off for a year with the Delicious project that would include, amongst others, Andy Rourke. Of the band, Davis would bitchily state: "It's sounding really heavy and clubby. We've recruited a guitarist called Gary who used to play with King Of The Slums and a brilliant vocalist called Colin. He's really strong on melody...which is not something I've been used to. On the subject of Shaun, Davis stated: "I don't want to see or hear from him again."

Paul Ryder, meanwhile, had been working with Oriole's sister, Astrella and their musical collaborations had been seized upon by Jeff Jaquin, the American manager of Astrella's Dad, Donovan. In a somewhat unlikely nod towards showbiz, the pair had been recording demo's in L.A which, apparently, had started to sound a bit "spacey...a bit like Kate Bush."

In direct contrast to this sun-washed superstar scenario, Mark Day had returned to work for the Post Office.

CHAPTER 19

Black Grape

Kermit was here, there, and everywhere. In the Hacienda, on the streets of North Hulme, on Market Street. Kermit was always there from way, way back. Everyone knew Kermit. Everyone knew Kermit stories. Everyone knew that one day, this man, would turn into something important. He used to prefer to be called DJ La Freak - "my mother knows who I am, that is all that matters." He was quiet, reserved, polite and talented. There was always talent, an enigmatic talent flowing out of Kermit.

The story begins back in the early eighties, at Manchester's Legends nightspot, down where Princess Street dips into darkness, and Manchester's city centre slips into seediness. Legends was always more flash than cool, more glam than punk. Along with the Roxy Room at Pips, Legends would be the city's premier 'new romantic' hangout. A flashy, post-punk white boy palace, trendily sitting on the edge of Manchester's gay village. But on Wednesday nights in the early eighties, things would become different. Manchester grandmaster of Elektro, Greg Wilson, held hardcore funk sessions, sussed enough to educate even the hippest of dudes from old Hulme. For anyone with an ear for the hardest black sounds, this was the place to be. And it was wild, too, with a dance floor that resembled a mass rugby scrum. All the while, down the road, the Hacienda remained a vast, cold, empty shell, full of echo-ey indie sounds and a few straggly raincoated students. Greg Wilson was where it began and where Kermit would soak in his influences. As DJ La Freak, Kermit would man the decks and become involved with DJ Dangerous Hinds whereupon the two became the driving force behind the great 80's/90's Manchester rap team, The Ruthless Rap Assassins. Before that, however, Kermit was infamously linked with The Hacienda during a spell with a Manchester break-dance crew, Breaking Glass. This group featured in several video's for Mike Pickering's pre-M People band, T-Coy and would even appeared on a number of youth TV programmes like *The Oxford Road Show*. Kermit was a star before his time.

The Ruthless Rap Assassins fell together by accident. Kermit was living above Anderson in Hulme, and they would play tunes to each other. This soon evolved into something more serious and they began to perform at local college parties. Following an infamous appearance at a militant Housing Rights gig at the International Two venue, the duo drafted in the help of sister rappers, Kiss AMC (who included Kermit's sister, Ann Marie), and, after a spell in a London studio, released the classic Manchester dance floor twelve inch 'We Don't Care', a stunning slab of manic hip-hop thrash-rap. Although never destined to rise beyond white label format, it was the archetypal, pre-Madchester dance floor underground hit. Only A Guy Called Gerald's magnificent 'Voodoo Ray' could claim to have had a greater influence on the bands who gathered around the scene. After 'We Don't Care', The Ruthless Rap Assassins, expertly managed by the old man himself, Greg Wilson, pushed Kermit's career onto a new, higher plain. The Assassins were more than a mere stab at fame, and their small body of work, hugely influential in Manchester at the time, haunts the grooves in a hundred subsequent acts, Black Grape among them. For a while, if only in this locality, they seemed to be the hippest thing in the world.

The RRA were the logical manifestation of North Hulme, the soured Utopian dream of vast arching crescents, latterly teeming with social desperation and hopeful energy, almost in equal portions. Hulme, north or south, contains a wildly bohemian cocktail of musical styles and influences - parties there had, for decades, been renowned for providing the hippest, sharpest sounds around and one of the archetypal Hulme sights is a living room stacked full of LP's or multiple CD towers. The Ruthless Rap Assassins stood for all that was positive in Hulme and, rather than pursuing a dour socialistic slant, they wanted money and pride. Flash 'n' working class, true to the tradition, in fact, of Happy Mondays. For a while it looked as though they might be snapped up by Fourth And Broadway although, after falling out with Kiss AMC, they would eventually sign for EMI and proceeded to produce the aptly titled *Killer Album*, which re-defined British hip hop without seriously denting the charts. Eventually, sadly, they failed to break through into the mainstream, and even managed to fall out with Hulme: "We've moved out from Hulme now," stated Kermit, "There are smackheads all over the place. The students come down for three years and they just wreck the place. They don't give a shit. They live rough just so they can say they lived in a ghetto for three years. They have spray canned all over the place. Manchester's got the biggest campus in Europe so there are whole rows of them. That's why I had to get out. I have no equipment now, which I need. Without it, I'm fucked, but with the smackheads and that, I just had to get out. Maybe, getting out was the beginning of the end of the Assassins. It did feel like the end of something, like I had come to this barrier. Perhaps, something better was going to come along."

Shaun and Kermit's musical liaison began way back in the Mondays history. Before they had started to collapse, back in the days when Kermit would skulk around the Hacienda and a hundred other dressing rooms soundly trashed by Happy Mondays. Kermit was there, always, a bundle of fun, a party animal, famous for his enthusiasm and his lyrical prowess. Shaun had always admired Kermit. He was cool, so cool. Always with the right people. Kermit had 'the knowledge'. He would sell dope to Ryder. Good dope, too, not the cheap crap that so often came their way. Kermit was always true to his word. And,like a love affair taking place outside a marriage, a relationship with Kermit slowly formed, and began to overshadow the actually marriage...indeed, making the marriage seem dull by comparison. Kermit was, to some extent, the intensely green grass on the other side of the fence.

To Shaun Ryder, for some considerable time Kermit's smack splattered lifestyle seemed like the most fun. And there was more. Bez, such an undoubted judge of taste, always hugely respected Kermit and the R.R.A. As Shaun knew, full well, Bez was rarely wrong. How ironic, to see this new band forming, naturally, around Shaun and Bez, the only two members of Happy Mondays who couldn't play a note. How perfect.

Just as Happy Mondays had started to take themselves seriously as musicians, they split up, leaving the non-musical ones to begin the long, unlikely fight back. Musicians would be found. Bizarrely, Shaun had eventually fallen for Bez's unlikely streak of Thatcherite common sense and bought a house, but predictably he was now in in financial dire straits, with his building society threatening to repossess. He was taken in hand by husband and wife management team Nicholl and Dime - Gloria and Nik Nicholls would later claim to have payed for a set of demo's for this newly-formed band and to have bailed Ryder out of his pool of debt (Ryder denies this).

Whatever the truth, with help, financial or otherwise, a band slowly formed around this strange trio of Kermit, Bez and Shaun. Searching for a name, Shaun Ryder would stop off at a late night petrol station and purchase a sickly sweet fruit drink. A 'black grape' flavoured fruit drink. It was as simple as that. A band, a name, a management team, a songwriting partner - it was all very refreshing, like the drink. It was sweet and new. Few people would bet on their success, but Shaun Ryder knew. He just knew.

The Reverend Black Grape

Kermit and Shaun Ryder's songwriting partnership began as it was to continue. With rhythm tracks pumping and popping away the pair sank into a mass of daft, gangy bonhomie, powered by spliff after spliff, becoming increasingly intoxicated, increasingly surreal, increasingly hilarious. The method was both simple and effective. If they could make each other laugh and swiftly transfer their insane witterings on to tape, then a lyric, of sorts, might begin to pop through the mess: "Yeah, yeah, that's how we work," agreed Ryder, "that's how we got the lyric for 'Kelly's Heroes'. You know, it was just a load of dumb talk and suddenly, out it came. That one about Batman and Bruce Wayne - stupid fucking line, or what? It just sounded so fookin' great at the time we knew we just had to slam it down." In the time honoured tradition of the Ruthless Rap Assassins' North Hulme, Ryder and Kermit would also carry out spot raids on their own and friends' record collections. As Shaun would later admit, to *Ikon*'s Caitlin Moran: "Me and Kermit, we work upside down, inside out, back to front, it comes straight out of me record collection. We just twist it and distort it and fuck it up until no one recognises it, and we can't get sued for it. Other records are usually the trigger."

Reefer Madness

If the spiritual home of Happy Mondays was arguably Chicago, then the natural resting home of Black Grape would quite probably be Jamaica. As far back as the late fifties and early sixties, Jamaica's position as one of the main sources of influence to the best of British music has rarely been questioned. And for Ryder, fifteen years on the draw must have induced a longing to sample that 'boom' from close quarters, to drift along the hot beach, to succumb to the night time throb of the bass. It was a spiritual home, of sorts, it was the place chosen for Black Grape to make the all essential video accompaniment to the band's second single 'In The Name Of The Father'. And who were they to argue? It was, as they say, a tough job.

The Grape stayed at Ocho Rios, a shimmering and mostly luxurious resort on the edge of Montego Bay. A great place to stay and play and smoke endless spliffs. Heaven, or what? Sitting around in a hippy-ish fog, like those days at Deeply

Vale festival, high in the Rochdale hills, like those nights in the corner of Pips, or in The Hacienda dressing room. Black Grape in Jamaica. A hot dream. Shaun Ryder, for one, cut a comic figure as he attempted to stand up and wander in zig-zag manner across the patio, his eyes revolving like a zonked-out cartoon cat, his legs constantly giving way, all his blood, all his feeling having been drained away.

"Fucking hell man, Jamaican draw, man," he would stutter, between giggles, sighs and vague hand gestures. Then he would sit in the corner and remember the night before when, according to *NME*'s beauteous stalwart scribe, Barbara Ellen "three erotic dancers arrived to perform in the Jamaican hotel room. The tallest girl is wearing a PVC swimsuit and and thigh boots. A tacky blonde wig sits on her head, making a sharp contrast with her flawless black skin. To the booming music the girl works the room, writhing first against the furniture then the floor. At one point, she stands with her back to the three men watching her, and places one hand on her left buttock, jiggles it at high speed. At another, she undoes the right shoulder strap of her costume and exposes a breast. Finally, the girl walks over to the quietest, least interested of the men and sits astride his lap. Lowering her head until it is level with his, she moves forward, and gazes, first wantonly and then puzzledly, straight into the stoned, laughing eyes of Shaun Ryder." There was, rather disappointingly perhaps for the press entourage, an easily identifiable 'chill out' atmosphere to the Jamaican trip. Shaun and Bez preferred to remain slumped by the pool or on the sofa, discussing music, while simply soaking in the glorious, steamy vibe of Jamaica. What a band...what a place.

Kermit was a little more lively, forever uttering laborious sentences like "Let's go out...let's go and get drunk...let's taste the night life." He couldn't help it. Never could stay still, not for a minute, Always on the move, from first thing in the morning, when he would roll a spliff, turn the hi -fi on loud, super-loud and then get out and about. The video director for 'In The Name Of the Father' was, fittingly, Don Letts. The same Don Letts who, as a Rastafarian DJ in Ladbroke Grove in the mid-seventies, had significantly introduced dub reggae to the punk nights down the Roxy, thus causing reggae to sink straight into the cutting edge of British music. Not bad, considering he only originally used reggae because there just weren't enough punk records around. Letts had spent much of the cataclysmic years of '76 and '77 filming the punks of London, and the Rasta's who encouraged the crossover. Who better then, to capture the genre-free cultural mish mash of Black Grape? Who better than Letts to understand just what the hell this band were trying to do? Nobody better, and Black Grape knew it which is one reason why, during the course of the filming, they remained on their very best behaviour. Indeed, quite the antithesis of the Mondays in Barbados, they managed to crawl from their beds at dawn, crawl out on to the scorching beaches before slogging away in the midst of such orchidaceous local beauty.

Time off from Letts was spent mooching about, playing football and falling about in a state of general, light-hearted lunacy. Apart from Shaun Ryder, who preferred to sit stock-still by the pool, emitting an air of enigma, complete with darkened glasses and black T-shirt. Truth was that he couldn't move. He was, as someone noted at the time, continuously "blissfully stoned." Eeking out his existence by eating foil-wrapped fish from the local Ocho Rios burger king, breaking his spell only to chastise Kermit for sitting on his awfully expensive looking designer sunglasses.

There were other fashion problems, during the video shoot. Problems that would go hand in hand with Ryder's self-confessed 'flash git' persona. Someone, for instance, stalked the singer, someone had noticed his gear. Someone, out in the shadows, had enough taste to know a good thing when they saw it. And they did. They stole Ryder's stunning Commes Des Garcons jacket (worth £2,000) and his Gaultier jacket (also worth £2,000), his Stone Island sweater (£600) and three pairs of £120 trousers. "You try telling that to the insurance company and they won't believe you," he would later stress, "I ended up only getting three grand back....cunts."

There was, inevitably with the Grape, a great TV moment, something to snap in your video recorder and keep forever, like The Pistols promo film for 'Pretty Vacant', like Joy Division on BBC 2's *Something Else*. It was the moment when Black Grape, as the Monday's had before them, took the *Top Of The Pops* stage in front of the usual preening, high street-garbed schoolies. Black Grape on *Top Of The Pops*. No big deal. Until, of course, we reached the second verse of 'Reverend Black Grape', most of us expecting a savage little edit. But no! Perhaps it was a sign of the changing times, perhaps it was a mere slip up, but even Shaun Ryder seemed surprised to discover the line, "Go put on your Reebok's man, and go play fucking tennis," screaming from the screen with unnerving clarity. Everyone heard it. "It were funny that," stated Ryder, "I kept expecting at rehearsals to be told to change it and no-one seemed to say anything. So I thought, well, they'll cut it out, somehow, but they didn't. And nobody really cared. If you had done that ten years before, idiots would have been kicking their TV screens in, wouldn't they?"

Of course, hidden, though not very well, in the lyrics to 'Reverend Black Grape' was another, rather more serious little outburst. Strong enough to attract hypocritical tabloid indignation. Strong enough to prize a comment from the Pope! Strong enough, perhaps, to cause serious friction in the Catholic masses of Salford? Possibly. "Old Pope he got the Nazi's to clean up their messes/In exchange for gold and paintings/he gave 'em new addresses." Ryder: "To be honest, me mam was a bit made up about all that. First of all it weren't half as worryin' as some of the other stuff that had been in the 'papers about me and, more importantly, all her neighbours' kids are in trouble for thievin' an that. So to have her son in trouble with the Pope, that's quite impressive for a Catholic. Not many folk can say that the Pope knows who yer son is, can they?"

Shaun Ryder: "The first Black Grape album....recording it didn't exactly help our attempts to stay clear of the old chemicals. When we started recording, we was just doing a bit of skank an' that. But things soon began to harden a bit. I suppose we started to feel the pressure. That's the killer with this business, suddenly you find that you are in a position where you have it all to do and to cope you begin to slide into...well, you know. Things started to get a bit naughty again as that recording was proceeding and we started partyin'. But after that I straightened up again. Not even any charlie or anything." Which rather makes a mockery of the album title *It's Great When You're Straight...Yeah*. Then again, all things are relative. What is interesting is the fact that, in order to achieve the final push, the famous last burst of creativity, a taste of party had to be induced. And it *had* to be, for the album was absolutely bubbling with the taste of party, a sublime 'upness', an album where the deepest thoughts were scattered across bubble and pop funk, and lovely duel voice interplay. Brash, clumsy and mad word play - but believable. That, in essence, was the album's true saving grace. The fact that, even if you do regard the sentiments as naive, you could forgive them because of their perfectly natural aura, their believable-ness. They might be wrong, but they *meant* it, maan. Wonderful. And with that in mind, the first Black Grape album slipped neatly away from the most obvious charges of flippancy.

CHAPTER 20

October 1995

The evening finished in a snap-happy paparazzi-style showbiz manner at Browns Nightclub in London's West End. A long way, one might think, from the GPO club in Little Hulton. There was Shaun Ryder, gold chain drooping arrogantly over his Lacoste T-shirt, more gold hanging over his wrists - "So what, I have always been a flash bastard, me," - draping his arm over the shoulder of Suggs, his mate for the night. It was a celebration for Black Grape and particularly for Shaun Ryder, who had in a professional sense finally 'come of age'.

Earlier in the evening the band had appeared on *Later With Jools Holland*. A good show, initially, that has quietly transformed into a great, perhaps the greatest of all televised popular music shows. It is especially welcome because of its simplicity in presenting musicians doing what they do best - playing music - and its overriding sense of being such a welcome antithesis to the 'yoof' and video age. Holland, whose presenting duties had started, somewhat ironically, with the ever chaotic Tube, had now become an icon of taste, even if his presentation style consisted of a hundred fluffed intros, liberally peppered with more 'Ladies and gentlemen' than you would find in an old time music hall. Everyone respected Jools, the supreme boogie man and all-round good egg. *Later* would effortlessly transcend taste and style, fashion and televisual gimmicks. Although there must surely have been a good deal of backstage ego clashing, not once has this ever been remotely apparent.

In a sense, the amiable atmosphere of *Later* would never have suited the Mondays. How could it? The effortless Black Grape appearance was proof of just how far Shaun and the lads had travelled. Here was Bez mixing with Gregory Isaacs, D'Angelo and Melissa Etheridge. "Yeah," stated Shaun, "I'm fucking pleased to be on *Later* because it's a top show, you know what I mean? I think the important thing is that Jools is presenting it, he's a top guy. And everyone sits around watching every one else's performance. It just makes the atmosphere really good, no question, and it's much better than most of the shit that gets on telly these days, by miles." A measure of a band? For sure. Grape performed three songs - all of which were infinitely superior to the versions they had attempted during their two hour soundcheck - 'Reverend Black Grape', 'In The Name Of The Father' and, to finish the show, a storming 'Tarmazi Party'. All performed with notable zest, a bouncing band beneath the giant blow up of Central Station's psychedelic Carlos The Jackal face.

Later, a cross legged, smoking, giggling Ryder would hold court in the dressing room, ignoring the feverish antics of a buoyant Bez, and obviously high on the show's infectious buzz. "I haven't enjoyed myself so much in...er...I don't think I've ever enjoyed being on TV so much. I hope the little thirteen years olds all watched it." And, on the same subject, to the *NME*, "If the thirteen or fourteen years old kids want to see the show, they'll see it, no matter how late it's on. I used to watch things like *Old Grey Whistle Test* when I was a kid. You just do. I don't give a fuck how old the kid is, he'll watch it if he wants to. If I was eight and I knew The Sex Pistols were coming on the telly I'd kick up such a stink, I'd have to watch it. *Later* is a live show and we've just played a live show tonight and people were there to see it. And with people like Gregory Isaacs there, watching as well, it's a top buzz."

The Smack Trap

Kermit, if has often been reported, had fallen into the smack trap, big style. Legend has it that he woke up one morning and heard his mother crying and that was the point when he decided, like Shaun before him, to quit the big H: "That was my turning point." Shaun would refute this: "Kermit's mother was upset all the time,, he has been making his mother cry since the womb. It made no difference to Kermit. He just said "sorry" and then went out and scored again. Other people can't make a difference. Not when you are like that."

That is indicative of just how bad Kermit was. Real bad. It had ceased to be recreational and had become essential. A daily occurrence. Kermit would soon be taking skag just to be able to feel straight and that was the point when he knew he was in serious trouble. That was the point when he decided to turn the corner. He had no choice. Like Ryder, it was either that or die: "It's not easy man" he would tell *Melody Maker*, "it's not fucking easy at all...but it's definitely the only way. It's definitely down to you. It's not like you wake up one morning and just stop. But you do wake up and realise what a total fucking mess you are." Like Shaun, Kermit opted for a slow come-down. Unlike Shaun, he would still admit to occasionally dabbling, as late as May 1995, by which time Shaun had completely banished the stuff from his life.

16 December 1995

Shaun Ryder was lying on a terracotta floor in Mexico, his torso bent into an ungainly L-shape, being sick. It wasn't serious, it just *felt* serious. A local bug. A little bastard of a thing had done it's dirty work and had taken Shaun Ryder out of the game just at the point when the game needed him most. What on earth was happening to Black Grape? Were they falling apart, physically, individually? Back in a Manchester hospital, Kermit was lying in a similar spoon-like fashion. Unlike Shaun, however, who would stumble to his feet, drink gallons of bottled water and would live to invade Cuba (more of that in a minute). Kermit's illness wasn't little at all...and it *was* serious.

He wasn't lying on a terracotta floor, but in an isolation unit, sealed in with the Aids and HIV sufferers, feeling like a condemned prisoner. His rock 'n' roll lifestyle, which he had dedicated his entire young life towards achieving, had been snatched away from him, just at the point when it all seemed to come together. Kermit had gone down with septacaemia, a disease caused by micro-organisms in the blood or, to put it more simply, blood poisoning. Nasty. Slices of his heart and liver had been flaking away. He had lost weight, up to two stone, and his poor, bent figure was pinned down by three intravenous drips. His public grapples with heroin were now cast into the shadows by something just as terrifying and not necessarily unconnected. Bez had been to visit him, taking along "some Amino acids and some ultra fuel...he hasn't got much muscle on him, now. You wouldn't recognise him, he's that thin. But he didn't want anyone to know. He kept saying "Bez, promise me you won't tell anyone I'm in hospital." Lucky it didn't happen while he was touring or he would have died. He would have been one of those...dead legends."

There had been an idea, in the wake of the good old United States refusing to allow The Grape to run rampant from shore to shore, to assemble the assorted Grapers in Cuba, in order to tease and charm the media darlings of America. It seemed like a good idea at the time. Inevitably, things became instantly blurred. Everything was set to go in Cuba, but Shaun was still in bloody Mexico. He had supposed to be relaxing, on holiday, chilling out although after four days, sweat had started to gush from his every pore.

Meanwhile, back in England, other things were happening. Bez, for example, was deep into a dream, in his bedroom at the Hilton Hotel at Stansted. The night before he had trundled through the watering holes of Bishop's Stortford. Missing the Havana flight wasn't, for once, Bez's fault. The hotel's computer had failed to issue the required alarm call and had formulated the opinion that Mr. Berry must have checked out. Bez snored on as a Cuban Air DC10, complete with a passenger list that included the *NME*'s Ted Kessler and omnipresent Salford snapper Kevin Cummins, roared over the hotel. The only Cuban flight, incidentally, to take off from Stansted in any given week.

The notion of Cuba was nothing short of inspired. Black Grape were not happy about being refused entry to the US - because of their criminal records...Jeeezus! What were the Americans afraid of? That Bez might subvert the angelic hordes of Queens, that Shaun might introduce a few bad habits to the gangsta rappers of Watts? Well, maybe. This time, America or, rather, the tiny section of American media that were actually interested in Black Grape, would have to travel to Shaun and Co. in Cuba. Where else? Well, it could have been slightly more ironic. They could have gathered together in Moscow and that had, at one point, been an option. The massed media ranks duly assembled over dinner, the Americans and the English, waiting, waiting. Eventually, miraculously, the band arrived. Their American-based A&R manager, Brenden Bourke, had gathered Shaun and Oriole Leitch in Mexico, and had whisked them on to the island. Bez, meanwhile, had been hurtled in via an enormously expensive excursion to Dusseldorf. Somehow, Shaun, Oriole and Bez managed to make an entrance at the same time in front of the somewhat startled gathering. If they had expected to see some kind of drug-fuelled freak show then, in a sense, they were not to be disappointed. Bez tore into view, filling the room with the obligatory obscenities, screaming to anyone who cared to listen about "Fucking nightmare fucking journey, fucking hotel computer, fucking turbulence, fucking hot maaan." Shaun meanwhile pumped a few arms before sitting opposite his girlfriend, straightening out, and looking like someone who had just spent a week curled up, retching on a terracotta floor in Mexico.

"Has anyone got any weed?" he screamed, "I haven't eaten or slept for three fucking days, I'm filled to fuck with antibiotics and I need a smoke, man." Now things,obviously, have changed within the American record industry. Long gone are the days when its very wheels were oiled by all manner of intoxication. Now its all gone horribly, horribly L.A. The assembled gathering looked down on Shaun with a mixture of guilt, confusion and pity. The looks were duly returned. No dope? No dope! For God's sake, if you can't score decent draw in Cuba, then you might as well resign yourself to a life spent sipping nowt but Croft Original on Christmas Day. With this in mind, Bez decided to take a trip out on to the streets to rectify the situation, pausing only to pick out a hovering white Rasta as his accomplice. It took just half an hour until, to Shaun's delight, a slab of something aromatic and Cuban was slapped in front of him. Good old Bez. And people wonder why Shaun always regarded him as such an important accomplice.

Leaving the building, Bez spied a beggar sitting in the entrance, holding two wooden blocks. Grasping these, Bez deftly performed an impromptu jig, complete with a surprisingly deft display of percussive block slapping, before handing them jauntily back to the beggar along with a £10 note. It was a touching little scene and the beggar, wished to instantly cement the start of an eternal friendship with Bez.

Duty called in Cuba, with Shaun and Bez holding court, initially with the English contingent of Kessler and Cummins who tactlessly pushed the subject of Black Grape's alleged continued allegiance with drugs. Great when you're straight? Who are you trying to kid? In London, around the time of the recent Black Grape Forum shows, it had been strongly rumoured that Bez had dipped for the first time (?) into heroin: "Nah," he stated, "the temptation's always there. Once an alcoholic always an alcoholic, same with drugs. So every day you have to say "no"." (No mention of the fact that this statement would seem to contradict Bez's refusal to dabble with heroin at all). "Some drugs were used on the tour though," admitted Shaun, "but I can honestly say that none of us have drug habits. None of us are dependent on drugs. I had a habit that I carried around for years but I've not had drugs for a while. I don't need them. I wouldn't change anything from the past, though. No way. We did what we set out to with the Mondays. I was the oldest, eighteen or nineteen and we had a couple of fifteen year olds in the band and all we wanted to do was live rock 'n' roll. We didn't get into the music biz to discover drugs and fuck about with instruments. We wanted a rock 'n' roll life instead of doing shitty little things and getting a wanky job. We wanted to stay out of prison. So living rock 'n' roll was cool. When you are in your thirties and you've got habits and you're fucked, rock 'n' roll needs a break from you and you need a break from rock 'n' roll."

A rather quaint little thing happened next. As Shaun was ushered towards the American press contingent, Brenden asked if he would like a drink. On hearing this, Oriole glanced towards him and offered, "Babe have a mineral water. You've only got one more day of anti-biotics and you've been doing so well. You can drink as much as you want tomorrow." Most of us know the feeling that produced Shaun Ryder's grimace at that point - when all reason simply vanishes and the only thing that matters is getting that damn drink. But Shaun obediently asked for a mineral water and attempted not to feel annoyed, as Oriole complained to the record company about the ridiculous idea of dragging Shaun to Cuba when he was clearly not well. Bored, tired, one hour later, she left.

Seizing the moment, Shaun turned around to face Bez. "Right dude," he gasped, "get the fucking brandies in. I feel like a drink." As it happened, inevitably, Shaun and Bez carried on downing brandies until three in the morning and, after such an enforced abstinence, awoke the next day with a volcanic hangover. Oriole, irritatingly enough, had been correct, for she knew full well that partaking of the odd snifter to ease the flow of the interview would inevitably finish twelve hours later in Bez's room blind drunk. Hardly the perfect preparation for a round of hugely important press and MTV interviews.

In a sense, Cuba was just about as near as Black Grape could get to the USA, at least, until record company muscle would procure some visas. The problem had occurred when the band had changed their passports from the lovely, tatty, large black and thoroughly British jobs of old, to the new lifeless little maroon numbers which, alas, carry a bar code in which is encoded a list of all the major misdemeanours of the holder. Somewhere along the line, the combined passports of Black Grape would read: drugs, drugs, drugs. Their surly faces hardly helped to dispel this extremely suspicious technology. Look at Bez - would you let this man into your country? Once in Cuba, they were pinned down and forced to answer the utterly banal questions of MTV. For example, isn't this simply the worst question in the world?

"Your music has been described in the US as Gangsta rave..."
Shaun: "That's a bad thing...it's bollocks."
Bez: 'First off, we are not gangsters. We don't go around shooting people and we don't make rave music."
Shaun: "We make music, gangsta's make money. Do you think I'd be sitting in Cuba doing a fucking MTV interview. I'd be in Cuba trading with the Columbians."

The daft question cut rather deeper than Shaun or Bez could know. For Black Grape had, indeed, been described as 'gangsta rave'. Not just once, not just via the stoned rantings of some fresh-out-of-high-school rock journo, or some jumped-up fanzine scribbler, not by some tuned off jock from the East L.A. suburbs, either...but by radio stations, hundreds of radio stations, across the country. From college radio to big time L.A. shows. One recalls the King of Sunset Strip, DJ Rodney Biggenheimer describing the Grape as "real Madchester gangsters." When you are described as a 'gangsta' in America, it does not compare with some daft, rock hack's description of a bunch of surly spotty oiks from Accrington. When you are called 'gangsta' in America, something sticks. Good for the image? Create a large, dark enigma? Maybe. Maybe America is big enough to house and hide a large number of scattered juveniles naive enough to believe such nonsense. Black Grape, from Manchester...baddest, meanest bad ass bastards on the planet? Every Black Grape and Happy Mondays fan and associate in England knows, full well, that these guys are, and always have been, puppy dogs in reality. Stoned, bladdered wittily subversive puppy dogs, but puppy dogs all the same. In England..it's a laugh.

In America it's not, necessarily, quite so amusing. People believe such claptrap and some of them, if only the tiniest fraction, are mad enough to act on it. Still, even the most horrific image can be papered over by clever clogs PR, and Black Grape's Havana interview was duly edited into ribbons, chopped into soft, neat little inoffensive soundbites until Shaun and Bez came across like a couple of Malibu surf punks who had dabbled with half a can of Bud and a Big Mac. Harmless and stupid which, frankly, is a big business kind of thing to be in the States. Fortunately, back in Blighty, we know a little better. Shaun Ryder and Bez and the rest of Black Grape are about as far from stupid as it's possible to get without alerting those who would so blandly over-intellectualise. Thankfully, Ryder and Berry remained quaintly eccentric in Havana. Think, for example, of their hired bus, trundling along, quite happily before screeching to a halt as Shaun Ryder leapt from the door, and disappeared into the admittedly evocative looking local barbershop. He emerged, twenty minutes later, sporting a severe No. 1 crop, much to the disbelief of the MTV crew. "I just see those clippers and they start whispering to me," explained Shaun, "They start whispering "Shave me, Shaun, Shave me, shave me", so I did."

Bez also surprised the on-lookers with this little unexpected outburst delivered, in the main, to the *NME* contingent: "You come to a place like Cuba and you wonder what the fuck the Americans are playing at. Like Clinton was in Belfast the other week, doing his saviour routine, preaching peace and goodwill while he's fuckin' starving Cuba to death. But it's alright, I'm just waiting for the West to collapse the way the communists have collapsed and, just the other day, America nearly went bust with a £370 trillion debt."

Shaun: "I thought that was pretty cool, man, Clinton's been giving all the dough away. But when Clinton goes to Belfast - and I'm not giving my views on the IRA here - he's a hypocrite. He's shaking hands with the IRA and he's got a big smile on his kipper and he's acting as if they are Jesse James or Robin Hood. But if it was Castro going over there he'd be going mental. Why can't he do the same for Castro.? Don't get us wrong, though, Ireland should be for the Irish and that's that. The Catholics should have what they want."

Bez: "It's not only the Catholics that live there. What about the protestants? You telling me that someone fourth generation Irish isn't Irish?"

Shaun: "They're Irish, but they're English. They support the Queen and the fucking British government. They're the ones who wanted the British troops there."

Bez: "You can't say that..."

Shaun: "They did, they wanted the troops there. But I'm not with Catholics or Protestants. I think everyone should live in peace. It's ridiculous that we are still arguing over religion in this fucking century. Religion was the first rule book, the first common-sense book to keep the species alive. Like, if you live in the desert you don't eat pork 'cos it will kill your insides, get rid of your foreskin. Make these fucking things up like, "thou shalt not do this, thou shalt not do that". Basically, the Bible was the first fuckin' police force. Now, we know a lot of this stuff like Noah taking two animals here, two animals there, couldn't have fucking happened. But there's a message there and we all go for the message. But in this day and age we've got to know that half of it is bollocks. It was just the first go at trying to be civilised. So why are we still arguing over this shit in the 21st. century? Everyone's just being tiny minded. These are traditions, let's treat them like traditions."

Bez: "Are we in the 21st. century now...or the 20th?"

CHAPTER 21

Imagine then, two blokes, in the seediest, ugliest, darkest corner of a Salford bar in the seediest, darkest, ugliest part of Salford. These two guys, mid-thirties now, were never actually dim or lacking in potential. They were, in fact, always quite bright but it was possibility, rather than potential, that slowly and cruelly drained away. The further away it drifted, the more difficult life became, sinking further and further into routine. Both of them, after a few years working for the Post Office, fell on to the soft, spongy mattress of the dole. Drifting there and back, each Wednesday, ignoring the patronising or bored stares from the DSS Staff. Drifting into the pub and then into their favourite corner. Drunken camaraderie, righting the world's wrongs, remembering that time when, pushed by some kind of blind optimism, they formed a pop group. No-one believed them. No-one ever believed any local group. "We are going to do this, we are going to do that." There was that moment when Phil Saxe tried to get Factory Records interested but the powers that be at Factory never made it to the Hacienda talent contest night. The band's situation just drifted on for a while before, inevitably, they split. They all see each other occasionally, but they are not really mates anymore. Still, when Shaun and Bez get together in the pub on Thursday afternoons, it's as if they have all the power and knowledge in the world, just chattering away.

Well, that's how it could so easily have turned out. The odds were massively in favour of casting Shaun and Bez into that darkened corner, to drift further and further into penniless alcoholism. Chattering away, all subjects covered, the saddest people on Earth. Not because they weren't intelligent but because their intelligence was never allowed to prosper. All the pubs in Salford, and Manchester and all the cities in Britain are still bubbling with the Shaun's and the Bez's who never quite got that break. In every watering hole in Britain, there are two friends, just like Shaun and Bez, talking about the same things, in the same way. The difference is, they always will.

Brats, Brats, Brats...Shaun Ryder, award beast. March 2nd, 1996

The Brat Awards. Shaun Ryder: "It's really nice to win an award, really nice. At one time I wouldn't have given a toss about it but it's very nice because it's voted by readers and all that lot. I sound like some daft old cunt, but it was nice to get the award. I've got nothing against awards, I mean, everyone wants to watch them, even though you think the fucker is fixed."

It was March, 1996 and Black Grape had won an award. Well, why not? The whole dumb, sham of Britpop seemed to be based on awards, hanging out, arguing, grabbing paparazzi shots and being a feisty female, or a bratty lad. So why not Black Grape? After all, this was the *NME*'s anti-awards award, their anti-paparazzi paparazzi event. Their anti-gossip gossipy event. God knows if it is meant to be a parody - at the end of the day, it is just the same as any other awards ceremony.

Jarvis was there. Noel was there. Goldie was there. Michael fucking Hutchence was there, and so too were Black Grape, making up with the *NME* after all these years. The band's 'Reverend Black Grape' had, against all expectations, captured the 'Single Of The Year Award'. Unfortunately voted by *NME* rather than, for some inexplicable reason, *NME* readers, but it didn't really matter. Black Grape are not the sort of band who normally win awards, so it made a nice change. Apart from that, it was a bloody good piss up and Black Grape, let's be honest, are hardly a band willing to pass up on such an occasion. The next morning, with a heavy cloud hanging over his forehead, Shaun Ryder appeared on the infamously loved, loathed, and now defunct Radio 1 *Chris Evans Breakfast Show*, No apologies for reproducing the interview here. Naturally, it makes fine reading:

Chris Evans: "Morning Shaun."
Shaun Ryder: "Hello Chris."
CE: "You alright?"
SR: "Yes."

CE: "Good night last night?"

SR: "Yeah, it was a pretty good night."

CE: "Take us through it. Tell us what happened. You were sat there waiting for your awards until 9pm. Then what?"

SR: "Well, I'll tell yer what happened then, Chris."

CE: "What happened then, Shaun?"

SR: "I come out of the awards thing to go over to the next club. And I got nicked."

CE: "You got arrested? What for?"

SR: "I don't know. I think I must have had, like, a dodgy face, or something."

CE: "Well Shaun, we all know you've got a dodgy face but it's not a criminal offense. You can't get arrested for having a dodgy face."

SR: "You can be arrested for having a big nose though."

CE: "Well, they don't come any bigger. Are you proud of your nose?"

SR: "I love it, me."

CE: "It's very useful, isn't it? A big nose in the rock 'n' roll industry?"

SR: "Yeah"

CE: "So did you have to go to the cells? Were you taken to the nick?"

SR: "Yeah, I was..."

CE: "Honest to god...this is true?"

SR: "Yeah, it was last night, remember, when we all moved from the awards..."

CE: "To the party?"

SR: "Well, it was only like ten yards to somewhere else. And in that ten yards I got nicked, you see. And the thing is, Oriole thinks I run off with some chick, so she hasn't been home all night 'cos she's been on one. Y'know, in a bad mood 'cos she thinks I gone off with some girl."

CE: "But you hadn't. You promise you hadn't."

SR: "I know I hadn't, man, fucking hell."

CE: "I gotta ask you about your mobile phone."

SR: "I lost it."

CE: "I know. You were dead keen, last night. Do you remember showing Michael Hutchence your new phone?"
SR: "Yeah."
CE: "And you said to us here, "Don't worry geezer, I've got a brand new mobile phone. Here's the number, call me tomorrow." So, at what point did you lose the mobile phone?"
SR: "Somewhere between going out and getting pinched by the busies. Er..whatever it was..must have been all that shandy I drunk."
CE: "What kind of mobile phone was it? Where did you get it from? Can we get you a new one? What kind of phone would you like and we'll get you a new one."
SR: "A nice small one."
CE: "A small one. A small mobile phone."
SR: "Yer."
CE: "And would you like us to get a small wrist chain, for it?"
SR: "How it comes."
CE: "Okay, we'll get you a new phone. What are Black Grape up to at the moment? Are you off on tour?"
SR: "Yeah, well, we just got back from Japan about...."
CE: "How's Kermit?"
SR: "He's getting better. They are releasing him. They were gonna let him out of hospital but now they've found he's got a hole in his heart."
CE: "Well, look, all our best to Kermit. We were taking bets last night about who was going to be released first, you from the nick or him from hospital. Thanks for talking to us. Have you got your award in your bedroom?"
SR: "You'll never believe this, Chris, I've lost it."

He had lost it, too, somewhere along the line. Black Grape's manager, Gloria Nicholls would later apologetically state: "He didn't lose his Brat through any lack of respect. It was a very proud moment in his life to get it because Black Grape have never won anything before. He lost it because he was like the rest of us on the night. Totally off his face."

In Sickness And In Health

There are those who believed, incredible as it may seem, that Kermit's disease had been exaggerated by the press, perhaps to gain mystique. There were those who saw Kermit, soon afterwards, in the spring of 1996, when his frame had whittled away to barely a twig, when his huge brown eyes sat, like massive targets on a gaunt, skeletal fizzog. Shortly before Christmas 1995, Kermit felt the soft brush of near-death, twice. His doctors later admitted that they had cast him off as a 'goner', that they had passed through all the dwindling stages of hope, until all that seemed left to do was to make him comfortable. He looked awful, as the *NME*'s Johnny Cigarettes discovered: "His head is shaved like an out-patient who has survived some terrible lobotomy experiment. His expression is constantly set in the mould of a shell-shocked child, whose natural hyper-active joie de vivre has been wiped out by some deep, untold trauma. He's seen the abyss that few in this life will ever have to experience."

I'd seen him, live with Black Grape, at Sheffield's Leadmill a year prior to this and it was Kermit's sharp, full-forced total enthusiasm that truly fired what was a remarkably electric set, a show simply brimming with the confidence of a band who had truly found their formula and were happy to ride and ride with it. Kermit would be snapping away at the mike like some deranged market trader, hurling words at an audience comprising of mainly tentative students who had never quite encountered anything like it before. Shaun was fun, that night, but Kermit had been dynamite. Perhaps that would be a dynamism that he would never fully regain. He was, after all, still so very ill. One of the valves in his heart had totally gone. The ventricles - the pipes to the heart - had broken off, so he was in a state of flux, waiting for an artificial valve to be put into place. He had to be careful...very careful. He was well enough, however, to join the rest of the band in Wiltshire, to help write and record 'England's Irie', with Joe Strummer, for the England Football Team Euro '96 campaign. It was a time, also, for reflection.

Kermit: "I used to think I was invincible. I've hardly ever been ill in me life before. I was always the one bouncing off the walls. I was always the last one to bed and the first one up. I had energy to spare, man, know what I mean? So it was like, erm, a bit of a shock, it makes you realise your own mortality....it's me own body that's fucked me up. All the years of abuse, man, it does catch up. I was one of the biggest drug monsters going, me. And I was still pretty naughty when I got ill, but not as bad as I used to be. I would have thought it would have happened to me a few years back when I was really tanning it bad, man. But I guess it's accumulation."

By this time it had been decided that Carl, Kermit's initially temporary live replacement, should stay in the band. It was Carl, or Psycho as he liked to be called, who seemed to thrive in the general 'chilling out' of Black Grape in the wake of Kermit's disease: "It helped a lot of people," he stressed, "'cos they saw Kermit, always the strongest, always the life and soul of the party and his body says, "oh yeah?" So the message is, sit down, chill out. Everyone in this band seemed to catch that vibe, man, you know, slow down guys, let's take it easy and enjoy ourselves."

Shaun Ryder. "I remember thinkin' "Fookin' hell me mate's in a bad way," we just wanted him to get better. Didn't have time to be thinkin' about ourselves. But now, believe it or not, I am pretty easy at the moment. My favourite thing at the moment is, like, just having a beer and a bit of weed. I don't really wanna do anything else, I just wanna concentrate on the music. I can do without caning it. Anyway, skunk's enough for anyone..."

There had been a tendency, it is true, as Black Grape stormed into contention, to regard Shaun, Kermit and Bez as a trio of drug freaks, burning up, perhaps, before storming out, big style. When the initial news of Kermit began to break, most would be forgiven for thinking that the time had come. Such thoughts were not only understandable, they would also haunt the band members involved. But that was to underestimate the strength of what brought them together in the first place. The fact that things had changed, that, perhaps as a result of simply managing to take greater control over their craft, the band had started to enjoy simply making music for music's sake. That Jools Holland appearance was no mistake. Black Grape had become, in the nicest possible way, 'musos'. The music would come first - before the drugs, before the sex, before anything.

Black Grape's likeable co-manager Muzzer would expand on this somewhat unexpected shift in direction: "Shaun can be such a funny bloke, brilliant conversation. Dead creative when he's straight. When he was on the gear he would just sit there, sayin' nowt. Staring at your shoes is no good for anyone."

Kermit: "We were all legacies of Thatcher's Britain. We all had to get off our arses. She made this country shit and if you didn't want to go down with all the other poor bastards, then you went out and hustled. Never say die, again, know what I mean? No surrender."

*   *   *

Happy Mondays, Black Grape, It goes on and on. They are still different, somehow. You have to go a long way from Salford to find something as enigmatic and as strange as Ryder. His strangeness continues apace - take, this example, in 1995, when Tony Wilson was desperate to locate the whereabouts of Derek Ryder. He rang the Ryder household and relayed a message via Mrs Ryder who, diligently, scribbled the words, Derek - Ring Tony." on the phone-side pad. An easy enough request. With this in mind, Wilson was confident that the call would be returned for the benefit of one of Derek's new bands. It wasn't. Refusing to bow to the indignancy of being ignored, Wilson called again. Again the note was scribbled down and it was made perfectly clear that it would be strongly in Derek Ryder's interest to return the call as soon as possible. No call came back. Eventually, just before Wilson was to finally lose patience, the two bumped into each other at a Manchester gig. "Why" asked Wilson, "haven't you been returning my calls?

Didn't you get the messages?

"What messages?" asked Ryder. The truth was soon revealed, and it was Shaun's fault. He had turned up one evening with a present for the family - a dog. Not just any old dog, but an Irish wolf-hound cross. The kind of dog one might have trouble containing on a farm, let alone a family semi. "But we always had dogs, mam," pleaded Shaun, as the hound snuffled off on its initial rampage. The Ryder's had always had dogs but spanials. The dog began to eat all kinds of previously inedible household items like, for instance, the phone pad. "The fucking dog kept eating the fucking phone pad," screamed an incredulous Wilson, "I mean, just how many important messages did that dog eat?"

February 1996

Shaun Ryder relaxes. He isn't in Manchester anymore, nor in London. He relaxes today in the Georgian farmhouse in County Cork, Eire, which he shares with Oriole. A white gem of a building set sweetly amid rolling lush pastures. Quite the antithesis of Little Hulton or rock 'n' roll. Here, a wild night is a few pints of Guinness down the local pub followed by a lounge on the sofa, a few spliffs and a *Deep Space Nine* video. A quiet life, indeed, where Christmas came and went in a blur of present giving - Oriole's two children share the idyll and occasionally some journalist or record company man or musician might drift in from that crazy world, far away. But the spell will not be broken, not for Shaun. Aged 34 and rising, his speakers still spit and pop with the latest funky craze - apparently, Houston's Geto Boys, a hardcore rap trio with little room for compromise. Chatting to *Select* magazine, Ryder would prove that, country idyll or not, he still has the hots for urban musical strife: "They are fuckin' great man. I love 'em. They've got it right. They've got the boom, man. You need the right tackle. You go back to the sixties and dig out their tunes. Funky as fuck, guitars on 'em, what people are doing now in the 90's. Everyone of the Geto Boys, Bushwick, Willie D and Scarface, every one of them can write great lyrics. They basically do it like I do. Schoolboy made up fuckin' rhymes. They're not glamourising violence, it's a comment on that sort of thing. You can listen to it and say 'double 'eavy' right. But, really, it's cartoon, man...I listen to this loads around the house. It makes you laugh, man. That's why I like it. Texas 'ip 'op. And it's naughty down there. They've just done another Geto Boys album and the fuckin' boom on their bass is the loudest you'll ever hear. I've always been a funky head. I can't help me taste in music, can I?"

CHAPTER 22

Stormy Weather

Even as Shaun relaxed through Christmas 1996 in his Irish idyll, mooching around to hip hop and planning to spend the next six months drinking Guinness and watching *Star Trek*, storm clouds were beginning to gather. A problem was occurring from Ryder's recent past. Ex-Black Grape management team Nicholl and Dime aka Gloria and Nik Nicholl, were threatening to sue Ryder for failing to cough up commission money totalling over £137,000, after Ryder had 'dropped' the duo back in June 1996. The couple claim to have resurrected Ryder's flagging career by securing the Black Grape record deal, and felt that Ryder had "acted disgracefully" by moving swiftly on to an elite Hollywood-based management company. In a tabloid story, depicting Gloria and Nik Nicholl living off benefit support, Ryder was duly condemned by them as "a bread-head...he loves money and must have thought why share it?" They alleged they paid for Grape's initial demo recordings as well as loaning Ryder £10,000 to pay off his mortgage arrears and save his house. Maybe, maybe not. It is all merely allegations.

Maybe Shaun, born opportunist, merely glimpsed the next step on the ladder and moved on. Maybe he has done that all the way down the line. Maybe that's why he ends this book reclining in domestic bliss, contemplating little more than his forthcoming purchase of a particularly flash Jaguar rather than, as a broken starlet, sinking back into Swinton obscurity and, perhaps, the waiting abyss of heroin. Not anymore. Ryder is out and proud, happy as Larry, with a hit band in tow. What's more, people are *interested* in Shaun Ryder. This man released very little music during the course of 1996 and yet still managed to command the front pages of a string of glossy magazines. He always seems to up the readership when he appears - because Shaun sells, people like Shaun. They want to know him. They want to know how it is done. The truth is, nobody knows how he managed it, not Tony Wilson, not Bez, not Derek Ryder and certainly not Shaun himself. He's a genuine phenomenon, perhaps the ultimate non-star. A non-enigma. The oddest star of the nineties.

DISCOGRAPHY

HAPPY MONDAYS

SINGLES

Factory FAC129	Forty Five EP: Delightful/This Feeling/Oasis	12"
Factory FAC142	Freaky Dancin'/The Egg	12"
Factory FAC142	Freaky Dancin'/The Egg (Mix)/Freaky Dancin' (Extended)	12"
Factory FAC176	Tart Tart/Little Matchstick Owen's Rap	12"
Factory FAC192	Twenty Four Hour Party People/Yahoo/ Wah Wah(Think Tank)	12"
Factory FAC212/7	Wrote For Luck/Boom	7"
Factory FAC212	Wrote For Luck (Dance Mix)/(Radio Mix) /(Club Mix)/Boom	12"
Factory FACD212	Wrote For Luck (Dance Mix)/(Radio Mix) /(Club Mix)/Boom	CD
Factory FAC222/7	Lazyitis - One Armed Boxer/Mad Cyril - Hello Girls.(A side with Karl Denver)	7"
Factory FAC222	Lazyitis - One Armed Boxer/Mad Cyril- Hello Girls	12"
Factory FAC222c	Lazyitis-One Armed Boxer/Mad Cyril- Hello Girls	Cass
Factory FAC232/7	W.F.L. (Vince Clarke Mix)/W.F.L 'Think About The Future' (The Paul Oakenfold Mix)	7"

Factory FAC232   W.F.L. (Vince Clarke Mix)/W.F.L. 'Think
                  About The Future' (The Paul Oakenfold
                  Mix)   12"

Factory FACD232   W.F.L. (Vince Clarke Mix)/W.F.L. 'Think
                  About The Future' (The Paul Oakenfold
                  Mix)/Lazyitis-One Armed Boxer CD

Factory FAC 242/7 Madchester Rave On EP. Hallelujah/Holy
                  Ghost/Clap Your Hands (Gatefold.
                  Limited Edition of 5000)   7"
Factory FAC242   Madchester Rave On EP   12"
Factory FAC242c   Madchester Rave One EP   Cass
Factory FACD242   Madchester Rave On EP   CD

Factory FAC242r/7 Hallelujah (The MacColl Mix)/(In Out
                  Mix)   7"
Factory FAC242r   Hallelujah(The Club Mix)/Rave On(Club
                  Mix)   12"
Factory FACD242r Hallelujah(The Club Mix)/Rave On(Club
                  Mix)   CD
Factory FAC242rC Hallelujah(The Club Mix)/Rave On(club
                  Mix)   Cass

Factory FAC272/7 Step On(Stuff It In Mix)/(One Louder
                  Mix)   7"
Factory FAC272   Step On(Stuff It In Mix)/(One Louder
                  Mix)   12"
Factory FAC272c   Step On (Stuff it in mix)/(One Louder
                  Mix)/(Twistin' My Melons Mix) Cass
Factory FACD272   Step On (Stuff It In Mix)/(One Louder
                  Mix)/(Twistin' My Melons Mix) CD

Factory FAC302   Kinky Afro/Kinky Afro Live/Kinky Afro
                  Euromix   12"

Factory FAC302r   Kinky Afro Euromix (Not UK)   12"

Factory FAC312   Loose Fit/Loose Fix (Perfecto 12
Mix)/Bob's Yer Uncle   12"

Factory FAC312c   Loose Fit/Loose Fix (Perfecto 12
Mix)/Bob's Yer Uncle/Hallelujah (The
Deadstock Mix)   12"

Factory FAC332   Judge Fudge/Tokoloshe Man   7"
Factory FAC332c   Judge Fudge/Tokoloshe Man/Bob's Yer
Uncle (Perfecto 12 mix)   Cass

Factory FAC62   Stinkin' Thinkin'/Sunshine And Love (A
Boys Own Mix)   12"
Factory FAC362   Stinkin Thinkin'Sunshine
And Love   12"

Factory FAC372   Sunshine And Love/Stayin' Alive
(Mix)/24 Hour Party People
(Remix)   12"

Strange Fruit SFPS077   The Peel Session: Tart Tart/Mad
Cyril/Do It Better   12"
Strange FruiT SFPACD077   The Peel Session   CD
Strange Fruit SFPSC077   The Peel Session   Cass

ALBUMS

Factory FACT 170   Squirrel & G-Man Twenty Four Hour
Party People Plastic Face Carnt Smile
(White Out) (First 5000, with palstic outer
sleeve, includes Desmond)
Tracks: Kuff Dam/Tart Tart/Energy/Russell/Weekends/Little
Matchstick/Owen/Oasis/Desmond/Cob 20

Factory FACT 170   Squirrell & G-Men Twenty Four Hour
Party People Plastic Face Carnt Smile
(White Out)(Reissue with Twenty Four
Hour Party People replacing Desmond)

Factory FACT 220   Bummed
Tracks: Country Song/Moving In With/Mad Cyril/Fat Lady
Wrestlers/Performance/Brain Dead/Wrote For Luck/Being A
Friend/Do It Better/Lazyitis

Factory FACT 320   Pills, Thrills And Bellyaches
Tracks: Kinky Afro/God's Cop/Donovan/Grandbags
Funaeral/Loose Fit/Denis And Lois/Bob's Yer Uncle/Step
On/Holiday/Harmony

Factory FACT 322   Live (Double LP)
Tracks: Hallelujah/Donovan/Kinky Afro/Clap Your
Hands/Loose Fit/Holiday/Rave On/E/Tokoloshe
Man/Denis And Lois/God's Cop/Step On/W.F.L.

Factory FACT 420   Yes Please
Tracks: Stinkin' Thinkin'/Monkey In The Family/Sunshine
And Love/Dustman/Angel/Cut 'Em Loose Bruce/Theme
From Netto/Love Child/Total Ringo/Cowboy Dave

Factory Once   Loads. The Best Of Happy Mondays
LONDON LC 7654
Tracks: Step On/W.F.L./Kinky Afro/Hallelujah - MacColl Mad
Mix/Mad Cyril/Lazyitis/Tokoloshe Man/Loose Fit/Bob's Yer
Uncle/Judge Fudge/Stinkin' Thinkin'/Sunshine And
Love/Angel/Tart Tart/Kuff Dam/24 Hour Party People

Factory Once Loads. The Best Of Happy Mondays
LONDON LC 7654 (Double Cassette with Loads More)
Loads More - Free with some CD's and all cassettes: Tracks:
Lazyitis (One Armed Boxer Mix)/W.F.L. (Perfecto Mix)/Bob's
Yer Uncle (Perfecto Mix)/Loose Fit (Perfecto Mix)/Hallelujah
(Deadstock Mix)/Freaky Dancin'/Delightful

Also:
Live Baby Big Head (bootleg)

BLACK GRAPE

SINGLES

Radioactive	RAD126	Reverend Black Grape/Straight Out Of Trumpton (Basement Tapes)	CD
Radioactive	RAD126	Reverend Black Grape/Straight Out Of Trumpton (Basement Tapes)	7"
Radioactive	RAD126	Reverend Black Grape (Dark Side Mix)(Dub Collar Mix)/Straight Out Of Trumpton (Basement Tapes)	12"
Radioactive	RAD144	In The Name Of The Father/Land Of A Thousand Kama Sutra Babies	CD
Radioactive	RAD144	In The Name Of The Father/Land Of A Thousand Kama Sutra Babies	7"
Radioactive	RAD144	In The Name Of The Father (A Chopper's Mix)(A Chopper Instrumental)/Land Of A Thousand Kama Sutra Babies	12"
Radioactive	RAD152	Kelly's Heroes (The Archibald Mix)/Little Bob (live)	CD
Radioactive	RAD152	Kelly's Heroes/The Milky Bar Kid Mix	12"

ALBUMS

Radioactive   RAD11224   It's Great When You're
                           Straight...Yeah
Tracks: Reverend Black Grape/In The Name Of The
Father/Tramazi Party/Kelly's Heroes/Yeah Yeah Brother/Big
Day In The North/Shake Well Before Opening/Shake Your
Money/Little Bob

Also:
Shaun Ryder featured on the single 'England's Irie' with Joe
Strummer and Keith Allen

INDEADENT MUSIC PRESS

BRITAIN'S LEADING ALTERNATIVE MUSIC PUBLISHER

OASIS: ROUND THEIR WAY - MICK MIDDLES

The first major biography of the Gallagher brothers and their masssive band. Includes fascinating pre-Oasis interviews and the full story of Noel and Liam's volatile relationship. Complete with an exhaustive discography and photographs from throughout the band's career.

128pgs with 15 photo's £9.95 + £1.00p+p

DIARY OF A ROCK 'N' ROLL STAR - IAN HUNTER

Widely regarded as the first rock autobiography and universally acclaimed as one of the finest ever insights into life on the road, this best-selling title is now re-printed for the first time in 15 years. Revealing the rigours of Mott The Hoople's enigmatic frontman, this is a landmark publication. *Q* magazine simply called it "the greatest music book ever written."

160pgs with 28 photo's £7.95 + £1.00p+p

THE PRODIGY - ELECTRONIC PUNKS

The official history of the world's most successful hard dance band, including hours of exclusive interviews with band members, families and friends, as well as photographs taken almost entirely from the band's own personal albums. *Electronic Punks* is IMP's biggest selling title and moved *NME* to call Martin Roach "the biographer of the indie heartland."

160pgs with 38 photo's £5.99 + £1p+p

POP BOOK NUMBER ONE - STEVE GULLICK

This fine collection of Steve Gullick's work from 1988-1995 captures the key figures in alternative world music. With rare and unpublished shots of Nirvana, Pearl Jam, Hole, Blur, Bjork, and many more, this is the most accomplished photo history of alternative music. *The Times* called it "one of the most beautiful and necessary books about 1990's pop and rock" whilst *Melody Maker* said "So stylish, so rockin'."

112pgs with 108 duo-tone photo's £12.95 + £1.50p+p   SOLD OUT

THE RIGHT TO IMAGINATION AND MADNESS
With an Introduction by John Peel
This landmark book provides lengthy interviews with 20 of the UK's top alternative songwriters including Johnny Marr, Ian McCulloch, Billy Bragg, Prodigy, Boo Radleys, The The, Pwei, MC4, Napalm Death, Wedding Present, Senseless Things, Utah Saints, BTTP, Aphex Twin, McNabb, Ride.

450pgs with 35 photo's £9.99 + £1.25 p+p

THE EIGHT LEGGED ATOMIC DUSTBIN WILL EAT ITSELF
The first and only detailed account of Stourbridge's finest, including previously unpublished photographs, exclusive interviews, a complete discography and reviewography, and an introduction by Clint Poppie. *Vox* described the début book and it's success as "phenomenal".

160pgs with 38 photo's £6.99 + £1p+p

THE MISSION: NAMES ARE FOR TOMBSTONES, BABY
The official and fully authorised biography of one of the UK's biggest goth bands. *Melody Maker* said "This makes Hammer of the Gods look like a Cliff Richard biog!", whilst *Record Collector* hailed "a tight fluid book which pulls no punches, an enviable degree of confidence, utterly compelling stuff."

288pgs with 38 photo's £6.99 + £1p+p

MEGA CITY FOUR: TALL STORIES & CREEPY CRAWLIES
This authorised biography is a comprehensive study of of this seminal band, containing 40 photographs taken from the band's own album, over 30 hours of interviews and a complete discography. *NME* said "its attention to detail is stunning."

208pgs with 40 photo's £6.99 + £1.00 p+p

THE BUZZCOCKS - THE COMPLETE HISTORY
The fully authorised biography of one of the prime movers of the original punk scene. Contains every gig, rehearsal, tour, record release and studio session the band ever played, and reveals rare unpublished photo's. *Q* declared it to be "an exhaustive documentation of these punk pop perfecto's that only prime mover Pete Shelley could improve upon."

160pgs with 25 photo's £8.95 + £1.25p+p

PLEASE MAKE CHEQUES/POSTAL ORDERS, INTERNATIONAL MONEY
ORDERS PAYABLE TO: *INDEPENDENT MUSIC PRESS*

AND SEND YOUR PAYMENTS TO: INDEPENDENT MUSIC PRESS,
P.O.BOX 3616, BETHNAL GREEN, LONDON E2 9LN
Please allow 30 days for delivery

YOU CAN ALSO ORDER VIA THE INTERNET:
http://www.rise.co.uk/imp